Unbleaching the Curriculum

Unbleaching the Curriculum

Enhancing Diversity, Equity, Inclusion, and Beyond in Schools and Society

Greg Wiggan, Annette Teasdell, Marcia J. Watson-Vandiver, and Sheikia Talley-Matthews

ROWMAN & LITTLEFIELD
Lanham • Boulder • New York • London

Published by Rowman & Littlefield
An imprint of The Rowman & Littlefield Publishing Group, Inc.

4501 Forbes Boulevard, Suite 200, Lanham, Maryland 20706
www.rowman.com

86-90 Paul Street, London EC2A 4NE, United Kingdom

Copyright © 2023 by Greg Wiggan, Annette Teasdell, Marcia J. Watson-Vandiver, and Sheikia Talley-Matthews

All rights reserved. No part of this book may be reproduced in any form or by any electronic or mechanical means, including information storage and retrieval systems, without written permission from the publisher, except by a reviewer who may quote passages in a review.

British Library Cataloguing in Publication Information Available

Library of Congress Cataloging-in-Publication Data Available

ISBN 9781475871005 (cloth) | ISBN 9781475871012 (pbk.) | ISBN 9781475871029 (epub)

We dedicate this work to a future generation. We are borrowing the earth from such a generation, and we hope that this contribution will help to make schools and society more humane and just for all.

Contents

Preface	ix
Acknowledgments	xi
Introduction: Enhancing Diversity, Equity, Inclusion, and Beyond in Schools and Society	xiii
Chapter 1: Unbleaching: Social and Historical Context and the Need for Curriculum Reform	1
Chapter 2: *The Teachings of PtahHotep*: Curricular Implications of the World's First Book	15
Chapter 3: Unbleaching Ancient Equations in Education: The Ahmes Papyrus, the Oldest Mathematical Manuscript	33
Chapter 4: "He Look Like Tupac!": Imhotep, the Father of Medicine	47
Chapter 5: The Olmec: Ancient Civilizations in the Americas	61
Chapter 6: Black and African Contributions in Asia and Europe	77
Chapter 7: Unbleaching: Contemporary Issues in Curriculum Design and Instruction	99
References	117
Index	141
About the Authors	145

Preface

This book investigates curriculum design, pedagogical omissions, and suppressed contributions of minoritized groups in schools and society to create greater diversity, equity, and inclusion (DEI). It addresses—and disrupts—the creation and maintenance of false binaries through *whitewashed* education, as well as in the curriculum in particular—for the preservation of power and privilege. As a correction for curricular omissions and the standard course of study in public schools, an *unbleaching* framework is presented that provides culturally inclusive practices that expand instructional and curricular based practices for all learners. This book is timely as it presents multicultural strategies through case studies that mitigate miseducation and *curriculum violence* to enhance instructional design, lesson planning, and inclusive classroom practices. The book presents DEI implications for education and beyond.

Acknowledgments

We wish to acknowledge our families and loved ones, as well as the enduring legacies and inspirational work of Drs. Carter G. Woodson, John Henrik Clarke, and Asa G. Hilliard III; Queen Nanny of Jamaica (Nana Asanti/Ashanti); and Ida B. Wells Barnett of the United States.

Introduction

Enhancing Diversity, Equity, Inclusion, and Beyond in Schools and Society

A people without the knowledge of their past history, origin and culture is like a tree without roots. If you have no confidence in self, you are twice defeated in the race of life.

—Marcus Garvey

Education can be a great source of social mobility, liberation, and *healing*. However, for many students, schools are institutions where they experience invisibility and are often excluded from the curriculum, disproportionately suspended and expelled, tracked into lower-level courses, and even forced out of school (A. G. Hilliard & Sizemore, 1984; Ighodaro & Wiggan, 2011; Morris, 2016). According to Watson-Vandiver and Wiggan (2021), the *healing power of education* refers to the realignment of curriculum and pedagogy to be inclusive, factual, and counter-hegemonic against dehumanization and its resultant social, psychological, and emotional damage and trauma. As such, school reform focusing on inclusion remains an area of major concern (Banks, 2010; Johnston, 2002; Neumann, 2013). Multiple efforts have been made to promote diverse school leadership, provide high-quality instruction, and improve student outcomes (Rury, 2012; Sleeter & Grant, 1999; Watson-Vandiver & Wiggan, 2021). However, less is known about effective school reform and curricular design.

As a core aspect of education, the curriculum can be viewed as the combination of lessons, practices, learning experiences, and student performance assessment taught in an academic program (Apple, 2004; Dreeben, 1968/2002; Johnston, 2002; Ladson-Billings, 2016; Marshall et al., 2007). However, when the curriculum reflects the contribution of all learners, it has a greater likelihood of empowering students and improving their outcomes (Banks, 2010; Gay, 2021; Ladson-Billings, 2016). In *Teaching to Transgress*, bell hooks, who was a monumental giant and contributor in the field of education and beyond, explains that traditional schooling maintains the orthodoxy. However, hooks argues that educators must be daring to transgress and disrupt the status quo (hooks, 2014). She states:

> To educate as the practice of freedom is a way of teaching that anyone can learn. That learning process comes easiest to those of us who teach who also believe that there is an aspect of our vocation that is sacred; who believe that our work is not merely to share information but to share in the intellectual and spiritual growth of our students. (p. 13)

In light of the life and contributions of bell hooks, *unbleaching* the curriculum helps us to transgress against systems of exclusions and oppression in education and beyond. Per hooks (2014), while the curriculum addresses the essence of knowledge, the question is whose knowledge is worth considering?

Generally in the United States (U.S.), those who hold political and economic power control the curriculum as an extension of that power. Thus, the curriculum tells us who is important and what is worth knowing as an extension of a dominant group. For those with power, to control the curriculum means to control the minds of learners. When minority students' cultural backgrounds and perspectives are excluded from the curriculum, they experience a sense of invisibility.

These omissions and suppressions can be harmful to all students, as they can create negative perceptions. However, when the curriculum is inclusive and considers the contributions of all humanity, everyone benefits. Curriculum reform can be the pathway for education as a source of healing and liberation. There is also a need for diverse perspectives and multiculturalism in curriculum development that reflects the changing dynamics of U.S. schools. Upon close analysis, trend data show modest school performance in our nation's public schools.

Underperformance is a major issue in U.S. public schools (National Assessment of Educational Progress [NAEP], 2022a, 2022b). Average mathematics and reading data indicate below-average proficiency across all school categories (NAEP, 2022a, 2022b). Meanwhile, projected enrollment trends show increasing diversity where minority students comprise the majority. Furthermore, the data illustrate that U.S. student demographics are projected to increase to 64% minority by 2060 (National Center for Education Statistics [NCES], 2020; U.S. Census Bureau, 2015). In fact, according to the U.S. Census, the multiracial population has increased by 276%, from 9 million people in 2010 to 33.8 million people in 2020 (U.S. Census, 2020).

Despite these changing demographics, White teachers represent 79% of the public school teacher workforce, and that number is expected to remain constant (NCES, 2020). Collectively, these challenges represent a need for an increased emphasis on diversity, equity, and inclusion (DEI) as central components of education processes and practices. This can also have positive impacts on student achievement.

U.S. school performance has been the subject of much discussion, which reveals a common theme of generally low proficiency levels. According to *The Nation's Report Card* (NAEP, 2022a, 2022b), overall, all school types (urban, town, rural, and suburban) scored below proficiency in mathematics and reading at both fourth- and eighth-grade levels. Based on *The Nation's Report Card*, 36% of students were proficient in fourth-grade mathematics assessments, while 64% were not (NAEP, 2022a). Similarly, only 26% of eighth graders performed at or above proficiency in mathematics, and 74% did not (NAEP, 2022a). In 2019, which was the most recent data available, 60% of twelfth graders performed at proficiency in mathematics, while 40% scored below (NAEP, 2022b). The reading scores were just as concerning. In 2022, only 33% of fourth-grade students were reading at or above proficiency, and 67% percent were not (NAEP, 2022b). In eighth grade, 31% were at or above proficiency in reading, and 69% were below proficiency. Based on the most recent data, in 2019, only 37% of twelfth graders performed at or above proficiency in reading, and 63% did not (NAEP, 2022b).

Taken together, the data above illustrate that student performance is a national concern and that there is a need for school reform (NAEP 2022a, 2022b). Given the COVID-19 pandemic (severe acute respiratory syndrome coronavirus 2, SARS-CoV-2) and its subsequent impact on educational delivery, these scores may continue to trend downward. In March 2020, when the U.S. entered into quarantine to prevent the spread of COVID-19, a significant number of students were impacted by remote learning plans that may have long-term effects on the students' educational attainment. Additionally, testing protocols were impacted by varying instructional delivery methods. Thus, the reliability and validity of scores for the period from March 2020 to the Fall 2021 return to in-person instruction are limited.

According to the U.S. Department of Education, National Center for Education Statistics (NCES), in 2018, the overall composition of U.S. public school students reflects an increase in minority students (i.e., Blacks, Latinx/"Hispanics," Asians, and others). Similarly, 2018 enrollment data indicate that more than half of Latinx, Black, and Pacific Islander students attended public schools where the combined minority enrollment was approximately 75% of the total school population (NCES, 2018).

Paradoxically, according to the U.S. Department of Education, National Center for Education Statistics, School and Staffing Survey, the percent distribution of teachers in public elementary and secondary schools does not reflect the diversity of the student population (NCES, 2020). In fact, as mentioned, in 2017–2018, the number of White teachers was 79% of the public school teacher workforce. This has changed slightly, as in the 1999–2000 school year, 84% of public school teachers were White, and only 8% were Black (NCES, 2020).

Collectively and in order to address DEI issues more deeply, the data indicate the need for a full review of educational processes and practices in U.S. schools. When students are exposed to a *corrected curriculum* that is historically accurate and inclusive, and when they receive the benefits of culturally responsive pedagogy (CRP), then the likelihood of academic success increases. CRP combined with a curriculum that is accurate, relevant, and appropriate, and whose educational processes are humane and democratic, can help improve student outcomes for all students (Banks, 2010; Gay, 2018; A. G. Hilliard & Sizemore, 1984; Ladson-Billings, 2009; Watson-Vandiver & Wiggan, 2018; Wiggan, 2008).

Given the need for U.S. schools to address a nationwide underperformance issue, an increasingly diverse public school population, and lack of diversity in the teacher workforce which remains majority White, more research is required to determine how this impacts curriculum development. While considerable research addresses why structural inequality arising from racism exists, and how CRP can help, more research is needed to address effective curricular design that improves educational outcomes for all students, but particularly underserved youth (Darling-Hammond et al., 2017; Freire, 1970/2018; Gay, 2018; Kendi, 2017; Kozol, 2005; Ladson-Billings & Tate, 1995; Love, 2019; Milner, 2012; Rickford, 2016; Rury, 2012; Wiggan, 2011b; Wilson, 2012).

In this sense, accurate knowledge is essential for expanding school-based instruction to ensure the healthy growth and development of all learners. In the quest for greater inclusion for marginalized groups, curriculum development is a major source for enhancing equity and excellence in education. Thus, a pervasive problem in today's schools is a curriculum that perpetuates cultural hegemony and omissions, and therefore requires unbleaching to correct and reposition it as a source of liberation (Byford & Russell, 2007; Ighodaro & Wiggan, 2011; Ladson-Billings, 2003; Watson-Vandiver & Wiggan, 2021; Wiggan, 2011b; Wiggan et al., 2014; Wiggan et al., 2020).

UNBLEACHING FRAMEWORK

Conceptual inspiration for this work and the framework of unbleaching comes largely from the residual legacies of slavery, colonialism, neocolonialism, and perhaps modern globalization, as world systems that privilege Whiteness against non-White identities. In the context of developing countries and particularly in Jamaica and other developing nations around the world, the social phenomenon of *whitening up* as internalized domination has been prevalent, and as such, a corrective framework is required. Hence, the process of *whitewashing* has impacted all two hundred countries in the world. In response to this, we believe the implications of unbleaching are relevant in every space, in every institution, and in every nation.

In the context of this book, *unbleaching is the process of disrupting Eurocentrism and systems of oppression that undermine, suppress, falsify, dehumanize, and marginalize non-Europeans and their perspectives and contributions as conduits for creating and maintaining power and privilege.* Unbleaching emphasizes changes in the conditions and outcomes of minoritized groups to challenge power and privilege and systems of exclusion, oppression, and marginalization in education and beyond (Wiggan, 2011b). In the context of education, unbleaching embeds DEI as core tenets of educational change, particularly in curriculum development, lesson planning, teacher pedagogy, school leadership, and student assessment. However, unbleaching is not anti-White or anti-European; rather, it is a purposeful process intended to dismantle systems of racial oppression, as well as falsification and omission surrounding minoritized people's contributions and perspectives.

In this sense, no one can control the parents they are born to, nor can they necessarily control the phenotypic characteristics they inherited. As noted above, between 2009 and 2020, the U.S. experienced a 276% increase in its multiracial population (U.S. Census, 2020). This underscores the need for DEI work in schools and beyond. Thus, unbleaching is not oppositional to any group, as all are viewed as part of the same human family tree. In this sense, it seeks to create greater inclusion by analyzing, critiquing, and disrupting systems of oppression that universalize the interests of one group over all others.

From a curricular perspective, unbleaching helps to upend *curriculum violence* and whitewashing in education to centralize DEI in all school processes. Curriculum violence refers to the deliberate manipulation of academic programming in a manner that ignores or compromises the intellectual and psychological well-being of learners (Ighodaro & Wiggan, 2011). It occurs when intentional or unintentional educational practices and processes compromise the academic outcomes of minority students. As J. E. King (2015) notes, racism can also be "dysconscious" in practice. That is, "dysconscious racism" is an uncritical habit of mind—involving attitudes, assumptions, and beliefs—that results in the justification of inequity and exploitation, which leads to acceptance of the existing order. Dysconsciousness, then, is a distorted perception of race.

Thus, unbleaching is a purposeful response to "dysconscious racism," *curricular violence*, and miseducation. It helps to mitigate Eurocentrism in education in general, as well as in curriculum development, which tells learners what is important and who is worth knowing. Miseducation, which has detrimental effects on all learners, refers to the indoctrination and the influence of European thinking under the guise of education (Woodson, 1933/2006). Thus, unbleaching corrects the curriculum and disrupts mythical master narratives about Europeans like Christopher Columbus and Amerigo Vespucci as discoverers and superior achievers.

In contrast, unbleaching critically examines systems of exclusion and Eurocentrism and positions DEI at the center of all educational practices and processes. Again, unbleaching is not anti-White or anti-European. It is a critical and reflexive process and practice that analyzes the ways in which the interests of the dominant group have been positioned as the basis of—and as referential for—human achievement, aesthetics, intelligence, and curricular and instructional design, at the expense of non-White perspectives and contributions. Thus, unbleaching as a process helps to create needed DEI principles in schools and society.

In this sense, unbleaching is not a minimalist attempt at add-ons to already racist institutional processes, systems, and curriculum design. In contrast, at its core, unbleaching dismantles exclusionary practices and falsifications to bring real and needed diverse perspectives and multiculturalism to school and curriculum development. In light of unbleaching, silence and falsification in curriculum and instruction is harmful to all learners. As such, specific attention is required to correct this.

Thus, unbleaching refers to a purposeful process and method of dismantling institutional and systemic hegemonic whitewashing in education and beyond. In light of this book, whitewashing is the process of suppressing, omitting, or falsifying history and social and educational content to support the interests of White-European cultural domination. Curriculum and instruction are central places where whitewashing and *bleaching* occur at the highest levels, as those who hold power control the minds of students. Relatedly, bleaching refers to the Europeanizing or Westernizing of social, political, economic, and educational institutions for the benefit of people of European descent. In this sense, the role of the media serves principally to advance the perspectives and ethos of the dominant group.

Through the process of bleaching, the presumption of White supremacy or White cultural leadership is foundational and becomes a pretext for advancing power and privilege. Per McIntosh (2002), White privilege is the unacknowledged benefits and advancements that Whites or people of European descent receive without having to earn them, but are rather embedded in society, as all things are measured against this dominant group. White privilege is often weaponized against non-Whites and used to gatekeep power and privilege. These behaviors become pervasive when there are no real systems of deep accountability, because those systems work in the interests of White privilege.

In fact, those who dare to complain about mistreatment and racial injustice may find themselves becoming super targets—to send a message to others that they will suffer a similar fate if they dare to try and create any meaningful change. In education, this manifests as centralizing Europe and European or White experiences and perspectives in curriculum and instruction, while marginalizing or even omitting minoritized groups. To advance DEI, educational systems and institutions must be unbleached, to ground needed multicultural perspectives. In response, unbleaching is the systemic and institutional work that disrupts Eurocentrism and hegemonic master-scripting that positions and transmits a dominant group's interest.

In the parlance of education, unbleaching uproots foundational assumptions regarding group supremacy that dehumanizes and marginalizes minority groups and their contributions and worldviews. In regard to the curriculum, unbleaching challenges falsifications and suppression in lesson planning, and it places at the core—rather than the margins—multicultural perspectives surrounding DEI as mandatory processes. Rather than working from a Eurocentric perspective, unbleaching grounds as foundational, multicultural perspectives and DEI as the basis of, and related purpose in, all educational work, inclusive of hiring, professional development, retention, promotion, school leadership, curriculum development, lesson planning, instruction, student treatment, etc. Unbleaching helps to ground DEI as the foundation of all educational processes and outcomes. In this way, unbleaching upends Eurocentrism, White supremacist ideology, and power and privilege in all educational processes and practices, inclusive of curriculum design and instruction.

Given the debates and attacks surrounding the use of critical race theory (CRT) and intense anti-Black and anti-minority posturing across the nation, unbleaching practices surrounding DEI speak to national needs in education and beyond. In light of the George Floyd case and other social injustices and civil unrest around the world, there has been increased activism related to antiracism work and DEI (Crenshaw, 2016). In Minneapolis, Minnesota, on Monday, May 25, 2020, in a world televised report, the reality of police brutality in the U.S. was on public display. America received international attention regarding the apparent mistreatment of Black people.

With a White police officer kneeling on his neck, George Floyd cried out that he could not breathe and eventually took his last breath as three other officers were standing by watching without offering any assistance (Henderson et al., 2020; E. Hill et al., 2020; Oppel & Barker, 2020). The reverberating reactions throughout the nation and around the world questioned these senseless police killings to understand why Blacks, in general, are treated so inhumanely in U.S. society. As a result of George Floyd, Jonathan Ferrell, and other cases of brutality and injustice, many institutions and organizations have published statements against racism. These public statements are a start, but they are not sufficient to effect change. A statement is not enough to do the deep and purposeful work to promote greater justice, equity, and healing.

Thus, unbleaching is a necessary process for creating changes in policy and practices, and in systems of accountability to increase DEI. Furthermore, current racial injustices surrounding Darryl Hunt, Ahmaud Arbery, Breonna Taylor, Keith Lamont Scott, and countless others, and the subsequent #BlackLivesMatter movement (a global nonviolent civil disobedience organization committed to building local power to intervene in violence against Black communities) shed light on the history of race relations in the U.S. (Garza, 2014). The election of the first African American president, Barack Obama (2009–2017), as well as the first Black female vice president, Kamala Harris (2021) (who is of South Asian and Jamaican descent), as part of President Joseph Biden's administration, suggest that there has been some progress. Notwithstanding these gains, racial tensions and mistrust remain very strong in the U.S.

The growing sense of activism surrounding social issues (the #BlackLivesMatter movement, the #SayHerName movement, etc.) has been effective in raising awareness regarding social justice issues, even resulting in strong turnouts during the 2020 presidential elections, where Black and Brown minorities came out to the polls in record numbers in support against what many perceived as a racist administration. Given these developments, it is necessary to provide social context for students in classrooms to discuss these DEI issues and to create spaces for healing, empowerment, and social transformation.

Perhaps by holding on to old traditions of exclusion and gatekeeping regarding power and oppression, some people feel threatened by discussions on race and White privilege. Legislation like House Bill 324 (HB 324) in North Carolina (and 27 other states), and its recent veto, has intensified conversations surrounding race, CRT, and its recent extension in *critical race structuralism* (CRS). CRS is a theoretical framework that analyzes social structures and institutions and seeks to liberate against racism and other forms of oppression (Ash & Wiggan, 2021; de Freitas et al., 2021; Wiggan, 2021; Wiggan et al., 2020). It analyzes racial and ethnic relations in social structures and institutions in terms of patterns and relationships between race, class, culture, gender, and structure.

Many states have responded to CRT with legislative actions. Entitled "Ensuring Dignity & Nondiscrimination/Schools," HB 324 sought to prohibit teachers from promoting 13 concepts, including the suggestion that America has a race problem or that some people are inherently racist or sexist (Pitkin, 2021). In its original language, HB 324 was designed to prohibit teaching that White people, or anyone else, have benefited from the actions of their forefathers. Governor Roy Cooper vetoed HB 324 in North Carolina. However, many states have embraced the legislation (Vaughan, 2021). In a September 2021 report, *Education Week* noted that the following states have signed laws restricting the teaching of CRT: South Carolina, New Hampshire, Idaho, Texas, Iowa, Oklahoma, Arizona, and Tennessee.

State education department officials in Tennessee threatened to withhold funds if schools violated the law restricting instruction related to CRT (Jeong, 2021). These actions reflect tensions surrounding race relations in the U.S. and speak to the need for DEI work in schools and society (*Education Week*, 2021). Given the events noted above, there is a need for unbleaching educational and institutional processes and discourse to create greater DEI practices around the country.

UNBLEACHING: UNDERSTANDING THE HUMAN FAMILY TREE

In the purview of unbleaching and issues of DEI and understanding our humanity, scientific research regarding the genealogy and origins of the human family tree can shed some needed light that helps to centralize this work (National Human Genome Research Institute, 2006/2011). Anthropology, archaeology, and science have provided evidence that East Africa—Ethiopia—is the birthplace of humanity (National Human Genome Research Institute, 2006/2011; Smedley & Smedley, 2005).

Additionally, science has proven that all humans share 99.9% of the same deoxyribonucleic acid (DNA) (Shared DNA, 2005). The mapping of the Human Genome Project shows that the 3 billion DNA base pairs are shared by all humans (National Human Genome Research Institute, 2006/2011; Smedley & Smedley, 2005). This suggests that we are more similar than different and that all 8 billion people who inhabit planet earth are indeed of African descent (United Nations, 2022). In regard to unbleaching, these scientific facts should be core understandings among all, as they help to upend group supremacy claims and racist ideology as a pretext for discriminatory practices and policies. Given these findings and our common human family, those who dehumanize and enact hate also inflict hurt on themselves and their humanity, as we are all members of the same family tree.

In the context of education and curriculum development, this is foundational knowledge that serves to unbleach orthodoxies of Eurocentrism and the dominant group's claims of superiority, as well as whitewashing through curricular design that underscores the myth of White supremacy. Further disrupting such myths, the origins of human civilizations suggest that some of the earliest ones are found along the River Nile in Africa, which is the longest river in the world (over four thousand miles long), where humans first started irrigation, farming, religion, the art of writing, architectural building designs, and schools (Morris, 2013). The Nile River flows south to north.

Going up the Nile River from Ethiopia, the birthplace of humanity, and then down into Kemet (Kemet was later called Egypt by the Greeks), the oldest book in the world, *The Teaching of PtahHotep*, was written around 2300 B.C.E. PtahHotep, who was a teacher and advisor to the Pharaoh, wrote what is regarded as the world's first book (Wiggan et al., 2022). In the purview of unbleaching the curriculum, this is foundational content that all students and teachers should know. However, given this important finding, the curriculum, both in K–12 and in higher education, remains generally silent.

Perhaps, per the orthodoxy of whitewashing in schools and society, White perspectives are standardized across the curriculum with a suggestion, albeit false, of having contributed all things that are worth knowing. Thus, the curriculum generally begins in Europe or someplace other than the birthplace of humanity and civilization, which is Africa (National Human Genome Research Institute, 2006/2011; Smedley & Smedley, 2005). For some who may falsely claim that beginning the human story at its origin in Africa is reversing the hegemony, such preposterous assertions speak to deep-seated conscious or unconscious bias, and even racism at times, under the pretext of, can any good thing come out of Africa or Black people?

However, learners should have knowledge that a person named PtahHotep, of African descent, who was a teacher, wrote the world's first book, and they should know the significance of that work as well as its educational implications (Myer 1900/2010). As we discuss in chapter 2, knowing and understanding the world's first book is important for all learners, not just Black and White, and it is foundational to the beginning of a cultural exchange of ideas and thoughts in the human experience (i.e., human history).

Similarly, moving down the same River Nile, an African named Imhotep, wrote the world's first medical manuscript. Imhotep is, in effect, the Father of Medicine (Hurry, 1926; Osler, 1921; Watson-Vandiver & Wiggan, 2018). As a vivid example of bleaching Black contributions and whitening up history, Imhotep's manuscript was renamed the Edwin Smith Papyrus in 1862 in honor of a European (Wilson, 1952). As we discuss in chapter 4, Imhotep's manuscript is still with us; however, it is generally known by the name of a European antiquities collector (Feldman & Goodrich, 1999; Meltzer & Sanchez, 2014).

In another case, the Ahmes Mathematical Papyrus, the oldest in the world, is misrepresented and largely omitted from school curricula (Akbar, 1998; Clarke, 1977; Diop, 1974; A. G. Hilliard et al., 1987). In this papyrus, Ahmes I (sometimes spelled Ahmose I) (circa 1550–1525 B.C.E.) provides the first evidence of advanced mathematics and analytics. As explained in chapter 3, the papyrus that originally bears his name has been renamed the Rhind Mathematical Papyrus, after Alexander Henry Rhind who purchased the work in 1858. To that end, there is very little mention of Ahmes, the true author of the manuscript, anywhere. This usurpation and renaming is symptomatic of Eurocentric practices that bleach or whiten up history to support White supremacist thinking. This is a tragedy, and the curriculum must become a central place of change, as this is where students learn crucial content regarding history and civic society.

In the parlance of unbleaching the curriculum, all students can benefit from *right knowledge*, as it correctly positions human and world contributions, and not at the expense of any other group. Thus, a corrected curriculum centers human diversity and contribution along a continuum of progress and with a focus on DEI. In light of this, as noted, science has shown that all humans are from the same family tree, which started in Africa (National Human Genome Research Institute, 2006/2011; Smedley & Smedley, 2005). The fact that all humans are of African descent could be a powerful tool of inclusion for all humanity, not just Blacks, and could help to further disrupt Eurocentrism in education and beyond.

ROAD MAP FOR THE BOOK

Thus, the purpose of this book is to present unbleaching as an educational framework that counters miseducation and curriculum violence to enhance DEI in schools and society. In chapter 1, "Unbleaching: Social and Historical Context and the Need for Curriculum Reform," we further explain the unbleaching framework and provide social and historical context regarding curricular reform. In chapter 2, "*The Teachings of PtahHotep*: Curricular Implications of the World's First Book," we present a case study of the oldest book in the world and address its omission and implications for expanding curriculum development. Chapter 3, "Unbleaching Ancient Equations in Education: The Ahmes Papyrus, the Oldest Mathematical Manuscript," discusses the contributions of the Ahmes Papyrus, later renamed the Rhind Manuscript, as one of the earliest mathematical documents, yet it is not mentioned in most educational spaces. In chapter 4, "'He Look Like Tupac!':

Imhotep, the Father of Medicine," we discuss the contributions of Imhotep as an example of curricular omission of one of the world's greatest contributors. Similarly, in chapter 5, "The Olmec: Ancient Civilizations in the Americas," we discuss the implications of the Olmec civilization as the oldest in the Americas and its significance for curriculum design and teacher pedagogy. Next, in chapter 6, "Black and African Contributions in Asia and Europe," we discuss early non-White contributions in Europe and Asia and their educational implications. In chapter 7, "Unbleaching: Contemporary Issues in Curriculum Design and Instruction," we provide recommendations for policy reform.

CHAPTER SUMMARY

In this chapter, we discussed the importance of DEI in the context of missing contributions in curriculum design, lesson planning, and teacher pedagogy in U.S. public schools. These omissions have serious implications for all learners, as stated content and school standards become a basis for what students across the entire country must learn. In the next chapter, we provide a social and historical context regarding Eurocentrism and the need for unbleaching.

Chapter 1

Unbleaching

Social and Historical Context and the Need for Curriculum Reform

> *Education is the most powerful weapon which you can use to change the world.*
>
> —Nelson Mandela

In the previous chapter, we introduced the unbleaching framework and discussed its implications for expanding DEI work in schools and beyond. In the current chapter, we explain the social and historical context regarding the need for curriculum reform to enhance teacher pedagogy and improve student outcomes. We begin by tracing the interconnections of the human family tree as a rationale for why unbleaching is beneficial for all learners.

As noted in the previous chapter, if all humans are of African descent (Shared DNA, 2005; Smedley & Smedley, 2018), how, then, could pseudoscientific racial categorization, anchored and embedded as it is in racism (Ash & Wiggan, 2018), ever serve as a proxy for deeper understandings about humanity when it is largely responsible for past and present disparities in education, economics, public policy, and society at large? And how could the false premise of *race* lead people to dangerous and harmful practices of *skin bleaching* as the internalized domination of White supremacy, and as a proxy for acquiescing to White privilege? Internalized domination and/or internalized racism can also arise in minority group members who embody racialized epithets surrounding minoritized groups and may hold similar racist views as a proxy for Whiteness, and even pose demeaning commentary when referring to other non-Whites. This is not okay or a pass on harmful words and/or behaviors that are racialized and are coming from other members of minority groups who have internalized White supremacist and racist master-scripting.

Indeed, this too is damaging and speaks to the harmful effects of racism and dehumanization.

Racialized internalization can also be exhibited in dangerous and hateful behaviors among oppressed groups exacted on each other, as powerless, fractured, and frustrated people, while holding fear and sometimes even private adulation for those with power and privilege, who might even oppress them and use their misunderstood behaviors as further legitimation for discriminating, eliminating, and having apathy toward these people, as well as what are perceived as Black and Brown problems (Native Americans and Latino/Latina). For example, in 2015, news outlets were filled with images of Dylann Roof who, in a mass shooting killed nine members at Mother Emanuel African Methodist Episcopal Church in South Carolina as members were joined in a prayer service (Chebrolu, 2020; Ibekwe, 2018). What was even more appalling was when viewers learned that after the perpetrator was apprehended on the scene for killing nine Black people, he was taken to a fast food restaurant (Burger King) by police officers to get food because he was apparently hungry (Elliott, 2020; Silverstein, 2015). The police officers were not discharged for this disgraceful conduct.

These senseless acts of hate, racism, and apathy surrounding Black lives illustrate the racial politics of the U.S. and its enduring legacies. Along with the social stigma and discrimination surrounding "non-Whiteness" imbued within the racial body politic in the U.S., Black and Brown individuals also endure the consequences of being undercounted and underserved regarding needed social and educational services. Notwithstanding these enduring legacies of racism, the concept of *race* is fairly new in the parlance of human history, as it is a social construction.

Given its ubiquitous nature, race is one of the hardest concepts to *unlearn*, as it has been embedded in all aspects of society and its institutions. Similarly, some may hold a common but incorrect belief that a religion can be a race. This too is inaccurate and requires *unlearning*, as a religion constitutes a set of beliefs and is not a race. Historically, powerful groups have often used religions to create false binaries between individuals and groups and even to discriminate based on a set of beliefs about the deities and even phenotypes, which are generally human conventions. In the parlance of race and racism, even members of the same religion can exact racism on each other, as the belief systems themselves and their related narratives are often a reflection of who has power and who were the historical conquerors.

As a point of context, a lesser-known fact is that the oldest religious book in the world is *The Book of the Coming Forth by Day* (2000 B.C.E.) (also mistakenly called *The Book of the Dead* by Europeans) (Budge, 1855/1967). Thus, unlearning is necessary, even though it can create discomfort and even cognitive dissonance. However, it is required to promote growth and development and to dismantle harmful and dehumanizing claims of group and/or even religious superiority. Race is a human creation or construction for which there is no scientific basis (Smedley & Smedley, 2005, 2018). It is the purposeful creation and maintenance of false binaries based on phenotype, for the production of—and preservation of—power and privilege.

For example, the "one-drop rule" was created to legislate Blackness in the U.S. and to gatekeep White privilege (Davis, 2010). The U.S. is particular and unique in its "one-drop rule," as all other societies appear to maintain some level of color stratification surrounding Black racialized body politics and color prejudice. Perhaps Brazil, which was historically the most lucrative colony of the Portuguese, is one of the most extreme cases of this, as well as imbued anti-Blackness (Nascimento, 2007; Wiggan, 2010). The degrees of coloration within Blackness carry high levels of significance even in the U.S. and across the globe. Hence, the rise of harmful practices of skin bleaching globally among Black and Brown people.

The politics of racism itself suggest that its practices are human conventions that can have detrimental effects on the life chances and outcomes of non-Whites. The case of Emmett Till, a 14-year-old African American boy who was lynched in Mississippi for supposedly staring at a White person, and countless others (Wells Barnett, 1895, 1900/2021), as well as the recent cases of Trayvon Martin, Ahmaud Arbery, George Floyd, etc., illustrates the pernicious boundaries and perils of U.S. racial and ethnic relations (Henderson et al., 2020; E. Hill et al., 2020; Oppel & Barker, 2020). In 2021, the U.S. Justice Department closed the investigation into Emmett Till's murder after supposedly failing to prove that the key witness lied (Jarrett, 2021). Even though the murder was well documented in media coverage, the judge ruled that no one could be prosecuted at the federal level based on the evidence available and given the statute of limitations.

The killings of Emmett Till and other more recent cases noted above, George Floyd, Ahmaud Arbery, and others, speak to the tensions surrounding America's racial and ethnic relations. In the book *Racial Formation in the United States*, Omi and Winant (2014) have provided some effective documentation regarding the evolution of race and Whiteness in the U.S. They illustrate how groups such as the Irish, Italians, European Jews, etc., who were not considered White (as White in North America meant to be of Anglo-Saxton descent), have evolved under a definition of Whiteness to later be considered White in modern times. As there are privileges associated with Whiteness, there have been many attempts to try and make a science (pseudoscience) out of a social construction.

One example of such attempts to operationalize race through pseudoscience occurred in 1734 when King George II of England founded the Georg August University of Göttingen, Germany, as part of the supposed European

Enlightenment period (Neuberger, 1943; Phelps, 1954). However, this university would become the center of some of the most racist propaganda research, also called scientific racism (de la Croix & Stelter, 2021; Park, 2013; Rupp-Eisenreich, 2014). For example, Christoph Meiners and Johann Friedrich Blumenbach, both of Göttingen, would develop theories of race and racism, which described Black and Brown (Native Americans and Latino/Latina) people as being subhumans (Bernasconi, 2020; Rupp-Eisenreich, 2014; Wiggan, 2015). Generally, Meiners is credited with coining the word *Caucasian*. Meiners and Blumenbach both argued that each race had a separate origin and that Whites were superior to all human beings. Blumenbach even attempted to measure and demonstrate that the skull or cranium of human beings differed and that because of these differences, Whites were supposedly superior (Bernasconi, 2020; Rupp-Eisenreich, 2014). Furthermore, people like Friedrich August Wolf and Karl Müller argued that Blacks and Africans were savages (J. P. Jackson et al., 2005; Most, 1997). During this time, scientific racism was being set in motion through the work of universities (Bernasconi, 2020; Rupp-Eisenreich, 2014).

Similarly, in 1869, Francis Galton, generally considered the father of intelligence testing, suggested that intelligence is hereditary (Guthrie, 2004; Wiggan, 2007, 2011b). He proposed that intellectual ability was limited to elite White families. This belief would be formalized through pseudo-research and White supremacy teaching and testing. The legacy of Francis Galton's work (and others like Lewis Terman, Robert Yerkes, Charles Murray, and Richard J. Herrnstein) is the basis and foundation of standardized testing in schools (Wiggan, 2011a). Further illustrating institutional racism in American education and society, a racist propagandist work titled *The Bell Curve* was at one time one of the best-selling books in education, which laid a racist framework suggesting that intelligence was inherited, and so therefore some groups, Black and Brown specifically, had limited capacities.

Education for the New Frontier provides examples of racist practices that are postured as intelligence testing and student assessment (Wiggan, 2011a). Similarly, in *Even the Rat Was White*, Robert Guthrie (2004) explains the history of racism in mental testing in the U.S., which subsequently filtered into public school assessments (A. G. Hilliard, 2000; Wiggan, 2007). As preposterous as this claim was, it spoke to the sentiments and dispositions of many educators and citizens alike. Given these racialized dispositions, what harm might educators, administrators, and curriculum designers impute, intentionally or not, as dysconscious racism, on minority children?

In light of this, unbleaching is urgent and crucial to help mitigate harm and to create greater healing for our most vulnerable population, our children. According to the mission of the Children's Defense Fund (CDF), it is critically important "to ensure every child a Healthy Start, a Head Start, a Fair

Start, a Safe Start, and a Moral Start in life and successful passage to adulthood with the help of caring families and communities" (CDF, 2022). Due to the exceptional work of Marian Wright Edelman, founder and president emerita of the CDF, disadvantaged American children and families have been the center of her advocacy and work to provide access to opportunities to help them navigate the nation's perilous landscape.

RACISM AS A MENTAL HEALTH DISORDER

Given the racial and ethnic relations of the U.S. and its harmful outcomes, how then do social constructions of race create categorizations that dehumanize people as, in effect, members of the same human family tree, become masters of exacting discrimination and bias regarding gatekeeping and White master-scripting in schools and society? The social constructions of race create real-life challenges, barriers, and threats for non-Whites. In this way, racism can be thought of as a mental health disorder among those who hold power and use it to consciously or unconsciously oppress and create barriers for others they perceive as being phenotypically and/or biologically different. This can be done through overt or covert processes that dehumanize and block access and equity for minoritized groups.

Those who exhibit racist behavior may benefit economically, politically, and socially; however, such actions may be a reflection of inner turmoil, insecurity, hate, and a low level of humanity. In this sense, racism can be thought of as a mental health illness, among those who hold power and use it to oppress racial minorities for personal or group gain, and of which those who practice it must heal. In order for healing to occur, the perpetrators must acknowledge these actions. As such, and from the perspective of human mental health and cognition, racism, through the false premise of White supremacy, is a needed criterion within a revised American Psychiatric Association (APA) *Diagnostic and Statistical Manual of Mental Disorders* (*DSM-5*), which is generally silent on the matter. Where there is trauma, healing is required. The very fact that there is no specific mention or criterion for this in the *DSM-5* may itself speak to institutionalized racism. This is something that organizations like the Black Emotional and Mental Health Collective (BEAM) and the Black Mental Health Alliance (BMHA) are attempting to address. Notwithstanding, since the *DSM* is diagnostic guide in the field of mental health, it could benefit from a revision that specifically addresses racism, racial trauma, and culturally responsive counseling which could help the educational training and professional development of mental health care professionals and their clients/patients.

The unacknowledged (*DSM-5*) impacts and damages of racism are extensive and require specific attention and treatment both on behalf of the perpetrators and the victims. For example, in the early 1900s, Eko and Iko were the sideshow stage names of Albino twins George and Willie Muse, the grandsons of former slaves who were exhibited like animals in the human zoo of the Ringling Brothers' Barnum and Bailey Circus. As in the case of the George and Willie Muse twins, the dehumanization and treatment toward the brothers speaks to the mental health condition among those who practice racism. Similarly, Ota Benga, a Mbuti African, was placed on display as an "animal" in the monkey house of the Bronx Zoo in 1906 (Newkirk, 2015).

These racist acts illustrate the poor mental health condition of those who dehumanize others and make fallacious claims of cultural and/or racial superiority. As a further example of the perils of racism as a mental health condition, in the book *A Brief Account of the Destruction of the Indies*,

Figure 1.1. Ota Benga on Display in the Monkey House in the Bronx Zoo in 1906. (Source: Wikimedia Commons)

Bartolomé de las Casas (1689/1992) documents the extermination of Native populations in the Americas. According to de las Casas, within 15 years of European entry, the entire population of Native Americans was reduced by half. De las Casas would, however, recommend using Africans instead of Native Americans as slaves. Furthermore, illustrating the psychology of those who practice racism, in *The Last of the Tasmanians*, Davies (1974) documents the European genocide of all the Indigenous people on the island of Tasmania, which is located off the coast of Australia. After the invasion, not one Indigenous person was left alive.

In North America, the forced breeding and sale of Blacks was a central basis of the economy. Sojourner Truth explains that all 13 of her babies were sold off as soon as they were weaned, and with the exception of one, she would never see them again (Truth, 1850/1998). Throughout the 20th century, across the nation, the widespread lynching of African American men was commonplace (Wells-Barnett, 1895). As a pretext for lynching, fallacious narratives of miscegenation were used as legitimation. Perhaps as enduring legacies, as mentioned, the recent killings of George Floyd, Ahmaud Arbery, Breonna Taylor, Keith Lamont Scott, and Jonathan Ferrell illustrate racism as a mental condition and its consequences (Henderson et al., 2020; E. Hill et al., 2020; Oppel & Barker, 2020). These cases are discussed in greater detail in a later section of this chapter.

BLEACHING AND UNBLEACHING IN GLOBAL AND HISTORICAL CONTEXT

Due to the fact that Europeans colonized more than 80% of the entire world, White supremacist thinking and hegemony have been expansive around the globe (Hertslet, 1909). Hegemony is the social and cultural leadership exercised by the ruling or leading class (Gramsci, 1971). In this way, it is the universalization of the interests of one group over all other groups. Generally, there are biases against Black people in all Western societies. As early as 1884, in a conference in Berlin, Germany (Berlin Conference), European countries held a meeting to parcel up the entire continent of Africa as colonial territory, with no African country present (Hertslet, 1909). In the book *Map of Africa by Treaty*, Edward Hertslet (1909) has provided some primary source documentation on this meeting. In fact, the maps in the book show the contours of the territories each European country claimed as their own. Subsequently, Ethiopia was the only African country that was able to defeat a European superpower and remain uncolonized (Wynn et al., 2021).

Europeans not only colonized the land and the people but also information about history—bleached and whitewashed (Clarke, 1979).

There has been a purposeful whitening-up of history, human civilizations, and world contributions that must be acknowledged, addressed, and corrected to stop the harmful practice of curricular violence and the widespread miseducation among all learners, teachers included. Oppressed groups as subjects of conquest generally have European names, speak European languages, and often hold European worldviews as part of cultural appropriation—through a whitewashed curriculum that serves as a tool of socialization for all learners. Historically, minority people's names were imposed on them, as all were given the names of their conquerors or enslavers, and they typically get their sense of civilization, aesthetics, and cultural ethos as whitewashing from the dominant group.

In the purview of history, Black, Brown, and Indigenous people across the world were subjected to global institutions of slavery and colonialism, which were capitalistic enterprises that evolved into systems of racism, racial stratification, and colorism. This stratification places Whites at the top and Blacks at the very bottom, with Africa and African features and ethos being the most maligned. Due to this stigma, people who are racially mixed may sometimes even deny their Black or African ancestry to avoid racial sanctioning.

As evidence of global anti-Black politics and White privilege, today the harmful practice of skin bleaching is still common and pervasive in Black and Brown countries. Skin bleaching is extremely dangerous, as it harms the body and removes protection from the ultraviolet rays of the sun. It is associated with ailments such as dermatitis, poisoning, kidney and liver damage, etc. The mercury in skin-bleaching creams and pills are also known to damage the central nervous system. The prescription drug versions of these items are at even higher dosage and are even more harmful. The proliferation of skin-bleaching creams, pills, and other products and their use among men, women, and even children, speak to the internationalization of White supremacy thinking and internalized racism. In this sense, skin bleaching is also a psychologically conditioned reflex among the oppressed, who view Whiteness as a proxy for personal and social advancement, and Blackness and/or Brownness as associated with oppression, self-hate, and social struggle. The Kenneth and Mamie Clark doll studies that the National Association for the Advancement of Colored People (NAACP) attorney Thurgood Marshall presented as evidence in the infamous 1954 *Brown v. Board of Education* case speaks directly to the dangerous effects of White supremacist ideology and its harmful internalization among oppressed groups and their school-age children (Clark & Clark, 1950).

Given the above discussion, Eurocentric racialized views of achievement and aesthetics are quite paradoxical, as Africans or Blacks are the progenitors of all humans, and for most of human history, highly melanated people populated the earth (Howell, Johanson, & Wong, 2018; Johanson & Wong, 2010). In this sense, Black aesthetics were a standard-bearer for most of human history (Ellis, 1989; Wynn et al., 2021). To this point, the Greek historian Herodotus, who lived in the fourth century B.C.E., notes:

> The Ethiopians to whom this embassy was sent are said to be the tallest and handsomest men in the whole world. In their customs they differ greatly from the rest of mankind, and particularly in the way they choose their kings; for they find out the man who is the tallest of all the citizens, and of strength equal to his height, and appoint him to rule over them. (440 B.C.E./2014, Book I, p. 184)

As Herodotus notes, Ethiopians were considered the most handsome. We should note here that the word "Ethiopian" is a Greek word that means people with black or dark skin. As such, in antiquity, the word "Ethiopian" or "Ethiopic" was also used to denote Black people beyond the modern-day borders of the country Ethiopia. In this sense, through anthropology, archaeology, and science, we perhaps understand that for most of human history, the earth was populated by highly melanated people. Even today, most people whose historical ancestors lived along the earth's equatorial line have high levels of melanin, which in addition to its many benefits, acts as protection from the sun's ultraviolet rays. Today, most of the world's population remains highly melanated, as low levels of melanin can be understood as adaptation and recessive genes, not different races of people (Shared DNA, 2005; Smedley & Smedley, 2018). This in effect means that people who are generally called minorities are in fact the majority of the world's population.

Science suggests that only 50,000–60,000 years ago, humans migrated into Europe (Muttoni et al., 2010). This is fairly recent in the broader context of human history, with the first humans appearing in Africa around 4.2 million years ago (Muttoni et al., 2010). As such, the human diaspora began in Africa, as they migrated outward to populate the other continents. Due to the global domination of Europeans through the institutions of slavery and colonialism, in more modern times, the standards of aesthetics, intelligence, ethos, etc., have shifted toward Western and White supremacist ideological thinking. This type of thinking is often internalized in oppressed groups, as the most central part of their oppression was not just physical force via slavery and colonialism, but psychological conditioning for social control and domination.

In the book *The Wretched of the Earth*, Frantz Fanon (2007) has done some excellent documentation on this. Similarly, in *Decolonising the African Mind*, Chinweizu (1987) chronicles the impact of whitewashing the Black mind. To this end, specific practices of healing and unbleaching are needed

(Watson-Vandiver & Wiggan, 2021). As noted, in the parlance of the world, people who are classified as White or of European descent are actually a minority of the world's population (Krogstad, 2019). In this sense, most of the world's population is non-White, and thus the process of unbleaching Eurocentrism becomes crucial in all institutional processes and practices.

As science reveals that all humans are of African descent, human phenotypic differences can be understood as geographical adaptation and recessive gene mutations for survival purposes (Shared DNA, 2005; Smedley & Smedley, 2018). Thus, phenotype variations such as eye, hair, and skin color, and other features, do not constitute different races but are genetic and environmental adaptations as nature's survival mechanisms (National Human Genome Research Institute, 2006/2011; Smedley & Smedley, 2005). Given these facts, no ethnic group or culture is superior or inferior to any other group. In this way, unbleaching helps to disrupt the myth of White supremacy and allows us to see our common humanity, rather than emphasizing differences as a basis of marginalizing and discriminating against others as a source of exacting power and privilege.

Unbleaching can help us unpack bias, which is common among all humans, and raise awareness and build inclusive practices that mitigate against racism, ethnocentrism, and Eurocentrism in schools and beyond. As such, rather than oppressing non-Whites, we can help to make society more just and humane for all, not just some. In the context of this book, schools, a key pedagogical and socialization institution, become ground zero for beginning the process of unbleaching—in curriculum, instruction, lesson planning, assessment, school leadership, and all related educational practices.

UNBLEACHING TENETS AND PROCESSES AND THE EDUCATIONAL IMPLICATIONS

As noted previously, unbleaching is the process of disrupting Eurocentrism and systems of oppression that undermine, suppress, falsify, dehumanize, and marginalize non-Europeans and their perspectives and contributions as conduits for creating and maintaining power and privilege. In sum, the processes of unbleaching entail the following tenets and principles:

1. Unbleaching is the systemic and institutional work that disrupts Eurocentrism and hegemonic master-scripting that positions and transmits a dominant group's interests (White).
2. Rather than working from a Eurocentric perspective, unbleaching grounds as foundational, multicultural perspectives and DEI as the basis of—and related purpose in—all educational work, inclusive of

Social and Historical Context and the Need for Curriculum Reform   11

hiring, professional development, retention, promotion, leadership, curriculum development, lesson planning, instruction, assessment, student treatment, etc.
3. It is not a minimalist attempt at add-ons to already racist institutional processes and systems (and regarding education, school, and curriculum design), but foundationally unbleaching dismantles exclusionary practices and falsifications, to bring real and needed diverse perspectives and multiculturalism to school and curriculum development.
4. It is not anti-White or anti-European, but unbleaching is a critical and reflexive process and practice that analyzes the ways in which the interests of the dominant group have been positioned as the basis of—and as referential for—human achievement, aesthetics, intelligence, and curricular and instructional design, at the expense of non-White perspectives and contributions.
5. Science has proven that all humans share 99.9% of the same DNA. The mapping of the Human Genome Project shows that the 3 billion DNA base pairs are shared by all humans (National Human Genome Institute, 2006/2011; Smedley & Smedley, 2005). This suggests that we are more similar than different and that all 8 billion people who inhabit planet earth are indeed of African descent (United Nations, 2022).
6. Thus, racism can be thought of as a mental health disorder among those who hold power and use it to consciously or unconsciously oppress and create barriers for others they perceive as being phenotypically and/or biologically different.
7. Skin bleaching is also a psychological conditioned reflex among the oppressed, who view Whiteness as a proxy for personal and social advancement, and Blackness and/or Brownness as associated with oppression, even self-hate, and social struggle.
8. Unbleaching helps to disrupt the myth of White supremacy and allows us to see our common humanity, rather than emphasizing differences as a basis of marginalizing and discriminating against others as a source of exacting power and privilege. Unbleaching can help us unpack bias, which is common among all humans, and raise awareness and build inclusive practices that mitigate against racism, ethnocentrism, and Eurocentrism in schools and beyond.

Unbleaching has the potential to create greater DEI education processes and practices, as well as to transform schools from places where miseducation and curriculum violence are common to spaces of inclusion where diversity is embraced rather than penalized.

Thus, with unbleaching, education can be an instrument of liberation against oppressive systems. Since a key tenet of unbleaching is dismantling exclusionary practices and falsifications, it helps bring diverse perspectives and multiculturalism in school and curriculum development. When academic programming is deliberately manipulated in a manner that ignores or compromises the intellectual and psychological well-being of learners, this is a serious concern (Ighodaro & Wiggan, 2011). A hegemonic curriculum with dangerous omissions of key historical contributions of underrepresented groups often results in miseducation and contributes to internalized domination. A key issue facing U.S. schools is the promotion of a hidden curriculum (explicit messages used to convey appropriate values, beliefs, and behaviors to children) that excludes the contributions of minority groups while advancing a dominant narrative (D. Bell, 1995; deMarrais & LeCompte, 1999; Ighodaro & Wiggan, 2011; J. E. King & Swartz, 2018; Wiggan, 2011b;

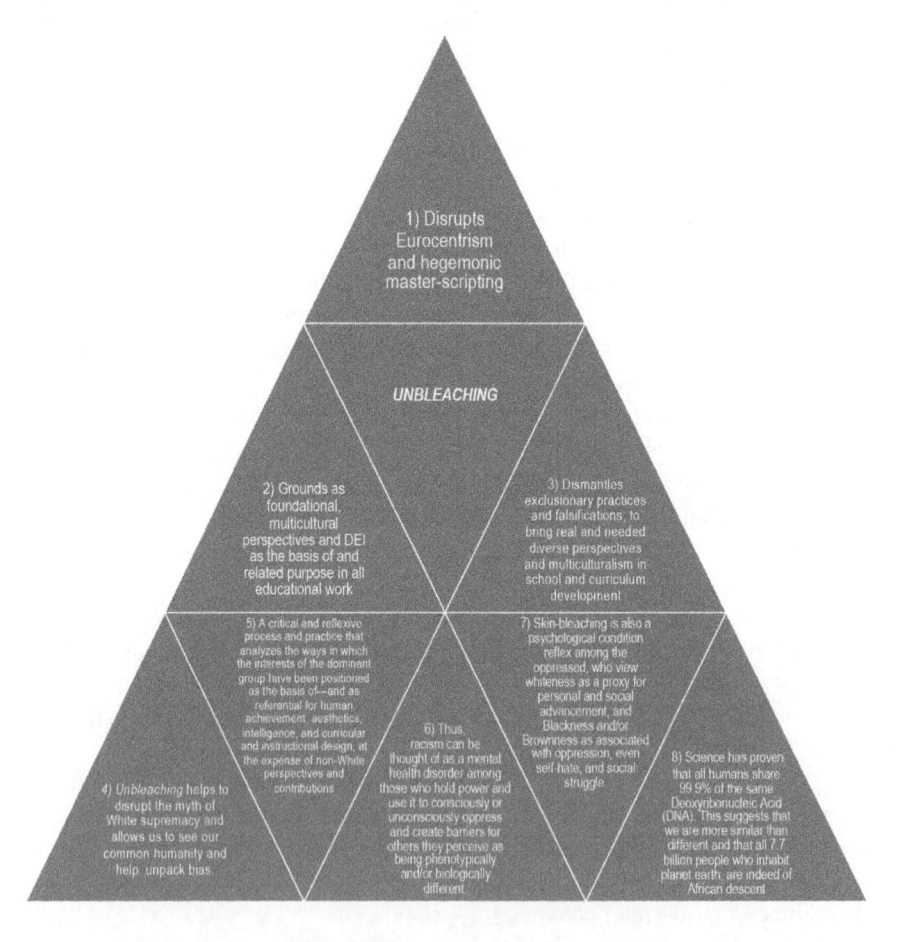

Figure 1.2. Unbleaching Conceptual Framework. (Source: Authors)

Woodson, 1933/2006). Incomplete accounts of human history focusing on the reference group are detrimental to today's learners and suggest the need for unbleaching (Ighodaro & Wiggan, 2011; Woodson, 1933/2006).

In the quest for equitable processes and practices in education, curriculum development is a major prescription for engaging equity and excellence (Banks, 2010; Grant, 2015; A. G. Hilliard & Sizemore, 1984; Ladson-Billings, 2009; Sleeter & Grant, 1987; Watson-Vandiver & Wiggan, 2018; Wiggan, 2008). Curriculum standards governing what is taught in U.S. schools are directly impacted by silence or distortions perpetuated through conscious or "dysconscious" racism which requires unbleaching and healing (J. E. King, 1991, 2015). The 1954 *Brown v. Board of Education* Supreme Court case legally outlawed separate but equal educational facilities, but it did not eradicate the ideological underpinnings of schooling that reinforced power relations (Kluger, 2011; Shujaa, 1994). Unbleaching the curriculum addresses the ways in which missing narratives promote internalized domination. It has the potential to disrupt what Adichie (2009) describes as the single story—one that begins at some point other than the beginning and that shows a people as only one thing over and over again. Those with power generally determine how stories are told, who tells them, and when they are told, which perpetuates the single story.

In spite of the above discussion regarding current controversies surrounding teaching about race relations, slavery, and critical race theory (CRT) in schools, recent litigation supports the infusion of the contributions of Blacks/Africans into the social studies curriculum. In 2002, with the passage of the Amistad Bill, New Jersey became one of the first states in the U.S. to make Black history a part of the core curriculum. In 2005, Philadelphia mandated that a Black history course be included as part of the graduation requirement. In 2020, the Texas State Board of Education approved African American studies courses as part of the standard curriculum (Grisby, 2020). Despite considerable controversy and the omitted contributions of certain historical figures (such as Malcolm X and Harriet Tubman), the changes are an indication of progress in curriculum development, yet further unbleaching is necessary.

Arkansas, Florida, Illinois, Mississippi, New Jersey, New York, and Rhode Island all have Black history mandates. Illinois requires public colleges and universities to offer Black history courses (L. J. King, 2017). These trends represent the importance of the inclusion of Black history in the general curriculum and not simply as separate subject areas. This directly relates to unbleaching, which is the systemic and institutional work that disrupts Eurocentrism and hegemonic master-scripting that transmits a dominant group's interests.

L. J. King (2017) has created a Developing Black Historical Consciousness (DBHC) Curriculum based on five principles: (1) power and oppression, (2) agency and perseverance, (3) Africa and the African Diaspora, (4) Black love and joy, and (5) modern connections and intersectional history. The state of Kentucky is implementing the DBHC Curriculum in its K–12 schools. To facilitate the implementation of these mandates, additional research is needed on effective professional development for teachers to apply a multicultural curriculum in schools. In this way, unbleaching dismantles exclusionary practices and falsifications to bring real and needed diverse perspectives to curriculum development.

Thus, this investigation addresses the gap in the literature regarding a *bleached curriculum* and its effects on K–12 education students (deMarrais & LeCompte, 1999) and the subsequent need for unbleaching, which can systematically disrupt Eurocentrism and hegemonic master-scripting that positions a dominant group's interests over others'. Using unbleaching as a conceptual framework based on eight core tenets, this book explores the educational implications of curricular omissions in U.S. schools and provides prescriptions and policy recommendations. Essentially, this book aims to unbleach the curriculum by grounding multicultural perspectives and DEI as the basis of educational work in U.S. schools. Unbleaching dismantles exclusionary practices and falsifications and omissions to provide multicultural perspectives rooted in DEI processes and practices.

Given the low student achievement levels noted in chapter 1, unbleaching offers needed school redesign in curriculum and instruction which could help improve the outcomes of all students. It systemically and purposefully dismantles institutional and systemic hegemonic whitewashing of the curriculum in U.S. public schools. Thus, unbleaching is the guiding framework that shapes the subsequent chapters of this book.

CHAPTER SUMMARY

This chapter examined national achievement levels and student performance in the U.S., as well as curriculum and development needs surrounding DEI. It laid the groundwork for unbleaching as the systemic and institutional work that disrupts Eurocentrism and hegemonic master-scripting in schools and society. It also provided the tenets and principles for unbleaching as a framework for the analysis, discussion, and recommendations that are to follow. In the next chapter, we address unbleaching and the curricular implications of *The Teachings of PtahHotep*, the oldest book in the world.

Chapter 2

The Teachings of PtahHotep
Curricular Implications of the World's First Book

Teach young people early on that in diversity, there is beauty and there is strength.

—Maya Angelou

Connecting to the previous chapter, which provided the social context for the unbleaching framework, this chapter presents a case study of *The Teachings of PtahHotep*, the oldest book in the world, and addresses its omission, as well as its importance for needed curriculum reform. In U.S. public schools, the curriculum generally reflects a single story that focuses on the dominant group (Adichie, 2009). This single story is typically whitewashed so that the contributions of minority groups are minimized or largely omitted. Unbleaching helps to create a solution for a curriculum that perpetuates cultural hegemony and miseducation (Byford & Russell, 2007; Ighodaro & Wiggan, 2011; Watson-Vandiver & Wiggan, 2020; Wiggan, 2011b; Wiggan et al., 2020; Woodson, 1933/2006). As noted in the previous chapter, unbleaching is the process of disrupting Eurocentrism and systems of oppression that undermine, suppress, falsify, dehumanize, and marginalize non-Europeans and their perspectives and contributions as conduits for creating and maintaining power and privilege. Unbleaching emphasizes changes in the conditions and outcomes of minoritized groups to mitigate against power and privilege, and systems of exclusion and marginalization in education and beyond (Wiggan, 2011a). In the context of education, unbleaching embeds DEI as core tenets of educational change, particularly in curriculum development, lesson planning, teacher pedagogy, school leadership, and student assessment. In the quest for greater inclusion for marginalized groups, curriculum development is a central component of enhancing equity and excellence in education. Thus, culturally responsive practices that are combined with a curriculum that is inclusive, relevant, and factual can increase student engagement and outcomes (Gay, 2018; A. G. Hilliard & Sizemore, 1984; Ladson-Billings, 2009; Patton et al., 2016; Rickford, 2016; Watson-Vandiver & Wiggan, 2018; Wiggan, 2008).

In 2018, the National Council for the Social Studies (NCSS) revised the *National Curriculum Standards for Social Studies: A Framework for Teaching, Learning, and Assessment*, which was an improvement. However, the standards leave noticeable voids in the historical record which could potentially contribute to miseducation (cultural indoctrination through improper schooling) (Akbar, 1998; NCSS, 2018; Woodson, 1933/2006). One such omission, *The Teachings of PtahHotep*, the oldest book in the world, holds implications for the revised social studies standards, curriculum development, and culturally responsive pedagogy (Gay, 2018; A. G. Hilliard et al., 1987; Ladson-Billings, 2009; Myer, 1900/2010; NCSS, 2018; Neumann, 2013; Ohito, 2019). To this glaring omission, how can teachers and students go through their entire educational careers and not know about the first book in the human record and its author, PtahHotep, who was a teacher?

Per the stated aims of the NCSS, social studies is supposed to provide coordinated, systematic study drawing upon such disciplines as philosophy, religion, sociology, anthropology, archaeology, economics, geography, history, law, political science, and psychology, as well as appropriate content from the humanities, mathematics, and natural sciences (NCSS, 2018). As such, a corrected curriculum should include and perhaps begin with PtahHotep and the world's first book. To this important point of inclusion and the work of DEI in schools and curriculum design, we are not reproducing the concept that there is one best canon. However, the omission of the world's first book is problematic. In the same way students learn about Greek thinkers like Herodotus and Aristotle, they are not apprised of PtahHotep, the author of the first book in the human record. Similarly, Ahmes, who wrote the oldest mathematical papyrus, and Imhotep, the Father of Medicine, are never mentioned.

In the case of the former, Egyptian (Kemetic) vizier PtahHotep (see Figure 2.1) wrote the oldest book in the world over 5,000 years ago. Today, this seminal work can be used in social studies classrooms to highlight the contributions of African civilizations as well as to supplement the social studies themes of culture, global connection, and time, continuity, and change (Carruthers, 1995; A. G. Hilliard, 1989; A. G. Hilliard et al., 1987; Myer, 1900/2010; NCSS, 2018). As such, unbleaching is necessary.

Due to the significance of PtahHotep as a central figure in African and world history as the person who wrote the oldest book, he should be included in the social studies curriculum and should be taught to all learners. The

Figure 2.1. Vizier PtahHotep. (Source: Wikimedia Commons)

historicity of the oldest book in the world affirms its correct placement within social studies—*civic competence*. Additionally, in the same way that all students gain from learning about Greek thinkers like Aristotle, Herodotus, Plutarch, Socrates, and Plato, they can benefit from unbleaching by also learning about PtahHotep (of Kemet or Egypt), the author of the world's first book. Egypt is home to one of the greatest civilizations humans have ever produced, and all students should be exposed to this (NCSS—*global connections*). In this sense, we are not arguing to remove the latter, but to include the former (PtahHotep), who is a precursor of all of these thinkers.

As the systemic and institutional work that disrupts Eurocentrism and hegemonic master-scripting, unbleaching grounds as foundational, multicultural perspectives and DEI as the basis of curriculum and instruction, lesson planning, and student assessment. Unbleaching dismantles exclusionary practices to bring real and needed diverse perspectives and multiculturalism in schools and curriculum development. Thus, the contributions of *The Teachings of PtahHotep*, the oldest book in the world, are an important aspect of unbleaching the curriculum. This is the world's first book, and it was written by a teacher; yet it remains virtually unknown in education discourse.

Appointed vizier by the Pharaoh of the Fifth Egyptian Dynasty, PtahHotep was a teacher, the highest-ranking official, and a spiritual advisor who wrote wisdom literature. PtahHotep lived during the reign of Menkauhor (2396–2388 B.C.E.) and Assa Djed-Ka-Ra (2388–2356 B.C.E.). He was a master teacher who used his maxims, which are preserved in his manuscript, to educate others and to improve Egyptian/Kemetic civilization. When the Greeks invaded and colonized Kemet in 332 B.C.E., they renamed the country Egypt. In this work, Egypt and Kemet are used interchangeably, as Kemet was the original African name, which means "Land of the Blacks" (Skelton, 2013).

This image of PtahHotep (see Figure 2.1) phenotypically supports Herodotus's report that the ancient Egyptians were Black (Herodotus, 440 B.C.E./2014). Furthermore, Herodotus notes: "It is certain that the natives of the country [meaning Egypt] are black with the heat" (Herodotus, 440 B.C.E./2014, p. 104). In *The Histories*, Herodotus acknowledges that Egypt is Kemet, the land of the Blacks. He notes, "My own conjectures were founded first on the fact that they [Egyptians] are black-skinned and have woolly hair" (Herodotus, 440 B.C.E./2014, p. 137). Similarly, the ancient Greek historian Diodorus addresses the intellectual acumen of ancient Egyptians. He describes their influence on the Greeks:

> But now that we have examined these matters, we must enumerate what Greeks, who have won fame for their wisdom and learning, visited Egypt in ancient times, in order to become acquainted with its customs and learning. For the priests of Egypt recount from the records of their sacred books that they were visited in early times by Orpheus, Musaeus, Melampus, and Daedalus, also by the poet Homer and Lycurgus of Sparta, later by Solon of Athens and the philosopher Plato, and that there also came Pythagoras of Samos and the mathematician Eudoxus, as well as Democritus of Abdera and Oenopides of Chios. As evidence for the visits of all these men they point in some cases to their statues and in others to places or buildings which bear their names, and they offer proofs from the branch of learning which each one of these men pursued, arguing that all the things for which they were admired among the Greeks were transferred from Egypt. (60/59 B.C.E./1790, Book I, p. 327)

Diodorus's observations are worth noting here, as he describes the Greeks and learning from Egyptians. He explains that Homer, Plato, and Pythagoras, among others, all studied and were influenced by Egyptians. As such, in the line of great Egyptian thinkers, who influenced many other thinkers, PtahHotep appears to have been the first.

In line to become Pharaoh, PtahHotep instead chose to pursue teaching and the priesthood, serving as the Pharaoh's chief official. His book, *The Teachings of PtahHotep*, written in MDW-NTR (pronounced "meh-doo neh-ter"), preserves "Africa and the world's oldest writing system" (Carruthers, 1995; Greppo, 1830; A. G. Hilliard et al., 1987, p. 8). Myer (1900/2010) reports that ancient Kemetic philosopher PtahHotep wrote the oldest book in the world circa 2300 B.C.E. in the ancient language MDW-NTR (the sacred writings or "divine words of God"), which the Greeks later called hieroglyphics. In spite of its historical importance, no information about *The Teachings of PtahHotep* is present in the United States social studies standards (NCSS, 2018). Please see the timeline of human history in Figure 2.2. Furthermore, African civilizations' contributions to world history have generally been marginalized, falsified, omitted, or whitewashed in public school curricula (Asante, 1990; J. E. King & Swartz, 2014; Watson-Vandiver & Wiggan, 2018). Thus, unbleaching is required.

Timeline of Human History
Human Family Tree and Development

4 million B.C.E.

[Dinknesh and Ardi — Ethiopia 3-4 million B.C.E.]

Cradle of civilization: human family tree

First book in the world: Teaching of PTAHHOTEP (2300) B.C.E.

First Written language Mdw-Neter

First university in the world Ip Ast University in Kamet (2000) B.C.E.

First book in the world: Teaching of PTAHHOTEP (2300) B.C.E.

Book of the Coming Forth by Day (2000) B.C.E.

Law of Hammurabi (1792) B.C.E.

Rig Vedas (1500-1300) B.C.E.

Odyssey and the Iliad (850) B.C.E.

Torah (700-500) B.C.E.

Septuagint (270-250) B.C.E.

Aeneid (20) B.C.E.

Figure 2.2. Timeline of Human History. (Source: Authors)

Unbleaching as a conceptual framework advocates for racial equity and social justice as a guiding lens. Thus, this chapter applies the College, Career, and Civic Life (C3) Framework to *The Teachings of PtahHotep* (Herczog, 2013a, 2013b, 2013c; Myer, 1900/2010). The *C3 Framework for Social Studies State Standards: Guidance for Enhancing the Rigor of K–12 Civics, Economics, Geography, and History* was designed to upgrade state standards and to assist practitioners in strengthening social studies programs (NCSS, 2017). Its objectives are as follows (Herczog, 2013b; Ingold, 2018; NCSS, 2017):

1. enhance the rigor of the social studies disciplines;
2. build critical-thinking, problem-solving, and participatory skills to become engaged citizens; and
3. align academic programs to the Common Core State Standards for English Language Arts and Literacy in History/Social Studies.

Using the C3 Framework and original documents from *The Teaching of PtahHotep*, this chapter examines the implications of the world's first book for social studies and education discourse (NCSS, 2017). We argue that PtahHotep's work helps to unbleach social studies and curriculum and instruction in public schools.

While several studies have addressed applying the C3 Framework to social studies lesson planning (Herczog, 2013a; Ingold, 2018; Long, 2017; Neel & Palmeri, 2017; Risinger, 2016; Zevin, 2015), no previous investigation has applied C3 to the oldest book in the world, *The Teachings of PtahHotep*. Hence, this chapter begins with a background addressing the revised *National Curriculum Standards for Social Studies* and the C3 Framework, then identifies ways in which *The Teachings of PtahHotep* can be incorporated in social studies discourse through the application of C3. Thus, the guiding question in this chapter is: *What are the curricular implications of The Teachings of PtahHotep for the revised social studies standards?* We begin with a discussion on theories of race and equity and the framework of unbleaching as a context for PtahHotep's work.

BACKGROUND ON CRT, CRS, AND UNBLEACHING

As noted in chapter 1, critical race theory (CRT) is a theoretical framework that agitates against racial and ethnic oppression and mitigates and liberates against racism. It advocates for racial and social justice as well as to mobilize marginalized groups to create racial equity and social and political change (G. C. Bell, 2017; Crenshaw et al., 1995; S. D. Dei & Lordan, 2016; Lorde,

1984; Martinez, 2014; Matsuda, 1991; Mertens, 2014; Ladson-Billings & Tate, 1995). CRT was coined by Derrick Bell, a constitutional law scholar, who developed the framework to analyze and explain society and culture as they relate to race, power, and the law (D. Bell, 1980, 2008; Crenshaw, 2001; Ladson-Billings & Tate, 1995). Bell (1995) notes five tenets of CRT: (1) counter-storytelling, (2) the permanence of racism, (3) Whiteness as property, (4) interest convergence, and (5) the critique of liberalism. CRT has been used as a theory to discuss a variety of social issues, and in education it has been applied to issues surrounding racism, student treatment, and desegregation efforts (Ladson-Billings, 1998).

Per CRT, racism is embedded in the legal system and in every institution, including education and state-mandated high-stakes testing (Crenshaw et al., 1995; S. D. Dei & Lordan, 2016; J. E. King & Swartz, 2014; Ladson-Billings & Tate, 1995; Martinez, 2014; Matsuda, 1991). In this sense, race and racism have been central aspects of the U.S. social, economic, political, and educational landscape. Thus, in the context of education, unbleaching is a purposeful and necessary practice to help promote DEI. As such, CRT and unbleaching provide a lens to analyze these processes and create change. Bell's concept of interest convergence is a crucial tenet of CRT (D. Bell, 1980), which helps to explain systems of racism. In this way, he argues that most Whites support racial progress or justice only in the sense that they will also benefit from legitimizing the oppressed or minority populations and cultures (D. Bell, 1980; Crenshaw, 2001; Delgado & Stefancic, 2017).

As an extension of CRT, critical race structuralism (CRS), as we mentioned in the previous chapter, analyzes social structures and institutions and seeks to liberate against racism and other forms of oppression (Ash & Wiggan, 2021; de Freitas et al., 2021; Wiggan, 2021; Wiggan et al., 2020). With a particular focus on schools, it frames racial and ethnic relations in social structures and institutions in terms of patterns and relationships between race, class, culture, gender, and structure. As such, CRT, CRS, and unbleaching agitate against and deconstruct Eurocentrism, Whiteness, and hegemonic indoctrination (Wiggan, 2011b). They help to liberate against hegemony or cultural dominance of one group over all others, as well as racialization in schools and society (deMarrais & LeCompte, 1999; Gramsci, 1971).

While not originally created as a framework to specifically examine education, CRT has evolved to become a transformative paradigm with a social justice lens through which social and racial disparities in schools are explored (D. Bell, 2004; Crenshaw et al., 1995; Delgado & Stefancic, 2017; Ladson-Billings & Tate, 1995; Lemert, 2004; Lynn & Dixon, 2013; Martinez, 2014; Matsuda, 1991; Mertens, 2014; Patton et al., 2016). Thus, with a particular focus on schools, unbleaching seeks to correct a curriculum that is hegemonic and supports a dominant narrative that excludes the contributions of diverse groups. Toward this end, teaching standards must be explored.

C3 AND CURRICULAR IMPLICATIONS OF *THE TEACHINGS OF PTAHHOTEP*

The NCSS revised the National Standards for the Preparation of Social Studies Teachers in March 2016, and it became available in January 2018 (NCSS, 2018). The *College, Career, and Civic Life (C3) Framework for Social Studies States Standards* (NCSS, 2017) incorporated purpose, preparation, and teacher practice with several key principles. First, social studies knowledge acquisition and application prepares youth for college, careers, and civic life. Secondly, at the heart of social studies is an inquiry of interwoven NCSS standards and teacher lesson planning that speak to the intersection of content and pedagogy (Herczog, 2013c; NCSS, 2017). Social studies also involves interdisciplinary applications. In addition, social studies emphasizes skills and practices for democratic participation and decision making, which has implications for students of all backgrounds (NCSS, 2018).

In spite of these revisions to both the NCSS standards and the C3 Framework, there is still a need for greater multiculturalism and a deeper focus on DEI to address curricular omissions (G. C. Bell, 2017; Crenshaw et al., 1995; Wiggan, 2011b). From an unbleaching perspective, the inclusion of works such as *The Teachings of PtahHotep*, the oldest book in the world, is crucial for all students, as it is one of the early works that begins the human written record.

C3 frames the NCSS revised curriculum standards to enhance the rigor of social studies education by building critical-thinking, problem-solving, and participatory skills that help students to become informed citizens (Herczog, 2013c; NCSS, 2017, 2018). In offering innovative approaches to engage students, C3 also supports student growth and development. Herczog (2013c) argues:

> Abundant research bears out the sad reality that fewer and fewer young people, particularly students of color and students in poverty, are receiving a high-quality social studies education, despite the central role of social studies in preparing students for the responsibility of citizenship. . . . Implementing the C3 Framework to teach students to be able to act in these ways—as citizens—significantly enhances their preparation for college and career. (p. 219)

The four dimensions of the C3 Framework promote inquiry and literacy in English language arts and history/social studies by (1) developing questions and planning inquiries, (2) applying disciplinary tools and concepts, (3) evaluating sources and using evidence, and (4) communicating conclusions and taking informed action (NCSS, 2017).

Upon close evaluation of the 5 standards, 10 themes, and 21 elements in the revised NCSS standards, the revisions do not adequately reflect a completely accurate representation of world knowledge. They also do not fully reflect a multicultural perspective that effectively serves students of color and students in poverty (Banks, 2010; Grant, 2015; Herczog 2013c; NCSS, 2018; Sleeter & Grant, 1987). Thus, an *unbleached curriculum* is necessary. As such, we contend that racism and hegemony are barriers to civic education (L. J. King, 2017). Specifically, the social studies themes of culture, global connection, and time, continuity, and change should include *The Teachings of PtahHotep* because they directly align with the key components of this text and offer insights for educators.

UNBLEACHING: CURRICULUM DEVELOPMENT

In the context of U.S. schools and overall low student performance discussed in chapter 1, the curriculum is an area requiring further study (Apple, 2004; Dreeben, 1968/2002; Johnston, 2002; Ladson-Billings, 2016). While the curriculum addresses epistemology or theories of knowledge, an underlying issue is who has power and what knowledge has been approved for learners (Byford & Russell, 2007). In this way, the curriculum can be viewed as a contested site of power and privilege, and, as such, unbleaching is necessary to create greater DEI. The NCSS publishes standards for the preparation of social studies teachers that outline social studies content, pedagogical knowledge, skills, and needed dispositions (NCSS, 2018). Competent use and mastery of all five standards are essential for effective social studies instruction. The C3 Framework facilitates alignment with the social studies standards and promotes inquiry-based instruction. The NCSS Core Competencies for Social Studies Teacher Education are as follows:

- **Standard 1, Content Knowledge:** Candidates demonstrate knowledge of social studies disciplines. Candidates are knowledgeable of disciplinary concepts, facts, and tools; structures of inquiry; and forms of representation.
- **Standard 2, Application of Content through Planning:** Candidates plan learning sequences that leverage social studies knowledge and literacies, technology and theory, and research to support the civic competence of learners.

- **Standard 3, Design and Implementation of Instruction and Assessment:** Candidates design and implement instruction and authentic assessments, informed by data literacy and learner self-assessment, that promote civic competence.
- **Standard 4, Social Studies Learners and Learning:** Candidates use knowledge of learners to plan and implement relevant and responsive pedagogy, create collaborative and interdisciplinary learning environments, and prepare learners to be informed advocates for an inclusive and equitable society.
- **Standard 5, Professional Responsibility and Informed Action:** Candidates reflect and expand upon their social studies knowledge, inquiry skills, and civic dispositions to advance social justice and promote human rights through informed action in schools and/or communities.

Several studies address the use of the C3 Framework to guide social studies instruction (Herczog, 2013a; Risinger, 2016). However, more research is needed to apply its use to primary documents such as the oldest book in the world (Ingold, 2018; Neel & Palmeri, 2017).

Herczog (2013b) offers an introduction to C3 by explaining its primary objectives and its applications to social studies curriculum standards. Revisions to C3 in 2017 align with this initial review. The central emphasis is on improving rigor, literacy skills, and Common Core State Standards (NCSS, 2017). According to Burns et al. (2019), a major challenge of 21st-century U.S. education is providing equitable access to deeper learning opportunities for historically underrepresented students. Deeper learning emphasizes critical-thinking, problem-solving, collaboration, and communication competencies. Similarly, Burns et al. (2019) find that California school districts that utilize comprehensive strategies yield higher student outcomes. Two common themes among the high-achieving school districts include support for collaborative inquiry-based instruction and better teacher preparation.

Neel and Palmeri (2017) offer recommendations for supporting preservice teachers and reforming teaching practices to apply the C3 Framework. In summary, preservice teachers need (1) content knowledge for teaching, (2) an understanding of the C3 Framework, (3) a vision for reform teaching, (4) chances to practice, (5) and venues to collaborate (Neel & Palmeri, 2017). In "Hacking the Middle School Social Studies Code," Ingold (2018) masterfully applies the C3 Framework by offering a reference table for enduring issues in social studies that combines formulaic and scientific approaches to concepts while also promoting literacy. Step by step, Ingold (2018) explains how the reference table for "Enduring Issues in Social Studies" opens up new ways of knowing for middle school students by making learning sequential, inquiry based, and fun.

Nevertheless, as the literature suggests, additional research is needed to help fill gaps pertaining to culturally responsive pedagogy and DEI in NCSS (Clabough et al., 2015; Dover et al., 2016; Gay, 2018). Thus, *The Teachings of PtahHotep* can help to expand social studies discourse and teacher pedagogy. Through unbleaching, this chapter provides implications for incorporating *The Teachings of PtahHotep* with the C3 Framework. Furthermore, it contributes to curriculum development by adding content that supports three NCSS themes: culture, global connection, and time, continuity, and change.

UNCOVERING *THE TEACHINGS OF PTAHHOTEP*

Considerable research explores the primacy of Africa as the cradle of civilization and *The Teachings of PtahHotep* as the oldest book in the world (Clarke, 1977, 1995; Diop, 1974; A. G. Hilliard et al., 1987; Ladson-Billings, 2009; Myer, 1900/2010). Therefore, the inclusion in social studies curriculum aligns with the themes of culture, global connection, and time, continuity, and change in the revised NCSS standards and supports an unbleaching emphasis on social justice in education (G. C. Bell, 2017; Crenshaw et al., 1995; Ladson-Billings & Tate, 1995; NCSS, 2018). This speaks to the limitations and possibilities of social studies education.

In light of our current inquiry, case studies provide a means for assessing the educational implications of *The Teachings of PtahHotep* for unbleaching social studies curriculum development. According to Merriam and Tisdell (2016), case study is "an in-depth description and analysis of a bounded system" (p. 37). Using *The Teachings of PtahHotep*, the world's oldest book, as a bounded case, this chapter helps guide curriculum development and application of the C3 Framework in Social Studies Education (Creswell & Poth, 2018). Additionally, critical content analysis is applied as a qualitative research tool to analyze the manuscript while making connections to social studies standards to determine the presence and meaning of concepts, terms, and words in written communication (Mayring, 2014). This systematic and replicable technique allows researchers to make inferences about the author, audience, culture, and time period (Mayring, 2014). From an unbleaching perspective, and as reflected in PtahHotep's writing, we examine the themes of culture, global connection, and time, continuity, and change within the social studies standards.

Due to its effectiveness in determining the themes and concepts of texts to infer meaning and messages, content analysis is also applied (Krippendorff, 2018; Mayring, 2014). This research method is used to review texts, and other data are interwoven to provide a thorough review of artifact(s) (Krippendorff, 2018; Leavy, 2007). Content analysis is an interpretive research technique for making replicable and valid inferences from texts to the broader contexts of their use (Krippendorff, 2018). It is the classification, tabulation, and evaluation of key symbols and themes in a body of communicated material.

Krippendorff (2018) identifies three distinguishing characteristics of content analysis. First, as an empirically grounded method that is exploratory in process and predictive or inferential in intent, it can be used to examine data, printed matter, images, sounds, and texts to understand what they mean to people. It also transcends traditional notions of symbols, contents, and intents. Contemporary content analysis has a methodology that enables researchers to plan, execute, communicate, reproduce, and critically evaluate. According to Hsieh and Shannon (2005), the three distinct types of content analysis are conventional content analysis (to describe a phenomenon), directed content analysis (to identify key concepts through using existing theory or prior research), and summative content analysis.

The content analysis framework (Krippendorff, 2018) demonstrates the main components. The researcher begins with a body of text, which is the raw data that is the source of analysis. Guided by the research question(s) used to examine the body of text, the content analysis is situated in context so that the researcher can analyze the work. In addition to content analysis, as a methodological approach, historical detection uses qualitative measurement and primary historical documents (Thies, 2002). This chapter applies the process of historical detection to analyze the oldest book in the world.

Following the tenets of conventional content analysis and historical detection, the artifacts used below are analyzed systematically. This replicable technique allows inferences about the artifacts and their time periods (Krippendorff, 2018; Mayring, 2014). We use primary source documents reflecting the original writings of PtahHotep (Myer, 1900/2010). Content analysis of the original plates written in the MDW-NTR (meaning "the sacred writings of the gods") from *The Teachings of PtahHotep* helps to provide evidence regarding its historical significance (Carruthers, 1995; Myer, 1900/2010). Below, we discuss our findings.

IMPLICATIONS OF THE OLDEST BOOK IN THE WORLD

According to Myer (1900/2010), the writings of the ancient Kemetic philosopher PtahHotep constitute the world's oldest book dated circa 2300 B.C.E. The papyrus from the original manuscript is examined as presented in Myer's *Oldest Books in the World* (1900/2010). Exposing today's students and scholars to evidence from the primary source and original plates showing the ancient writings in MDW-NTR is instructive. Furthermore, it aligns with Hilliard's (1989) reminder that seeing is better than hearing. Based on critical content analysis and an unbleaching framework, the documents are thematically analyzed and coded in relation to the themes of culture, global connection, and time, continuity, and change in the revised NCSS standards.

These writings underscore how "through the study of culture, and cultural diversity, learners understand how human beings create, learn, share, and adapt to culture, and appreciate the role of culture in shaping their lives and society, as well as the societies of others" (NCSS, 2018, p. 3). In light of the need for unbleaching and in connection with NCSS, greater DEI work is required. According to NCSS (2018), *global interdependence* is a theme that prepares students to analyze issues arising from globalization, meaning increasing interdependences and integration in the world's economic, social, and cultural systems (Monkman & Stromquist, 2000). It requires an understanding of the important and diverse global connections among world societies. This typically appears in units or courses pertaining to geography, culture, economics, history, political science, government, and technology. In those units, *The Teachings of PtahHotep* should appear.

The original papyrus from *The Teachings of PtahHotep* is currently on display in the British Museum. Revillout (in Myer 1900/2010) noted, "Among the monuments of the Valley of the Nile, established for eternity, none had more solid foundations than Egyptian wisdom" (p. 50). According to Myer (1900/2010), 90% of Kemetic papyri focus on "victory of Good over Evil, of Right over Wrong" (p. 32). Concerned with how to lead an ethical life, PtahHotep presents his knowledge and experiences in a didactic and reflective way in *The Teachings of PtahHotep* (Graness, 2016).

A close examination of the original manuscript from the world's oldest book (see Figure 2.3) can be connected to the NCSS standards with particular emphasis on the stated themes of culture, global connection, and time, continuity, and change. *The Teachings of PtahHotep* provides context for building knowledge through content-rich text. Beyond the original artifact held in the British Museum, Myer (1900/2010) records the original papyrus representing the "Beginning" and "Ending" of the book of PtahHotep.

Myer (1900/2010) presents the Plate III papyri showcasing the "Beginning" of the book of PtahHotep with an English translation that states: "From the Precepts of the Prefect, the Feudal Lord Ptah-Hotep Living Under the Majesty of the King of the South and the North, DAD-KA-RA or ASSA of the FIFTH EGYPTIAN DYNASTY" (ca. 3580–3536 B.C.E.). *The Teachings of PtahHotep* includes maxims further detailed in Myer (1900/2010) from the original papyri. Overall, they present foundational principles for human behavior that together represent one of the highest codes of conduct. This

Figure 2.3. The Prisse Papyrus. Egyptien 194, Teaching of Ptahhotep (596-end), right column. Middle Kingdom manuscript, 12th dynasty, c. 1800 BC. Inscribed in hieratic. (Source: Wikimedia Commons)

moral code connects to the NCSS themes of culture, global connection, and time, continuity, and change wherein learners:

> Examine the institutions, values, and beliefs of people in the past, acquire skills in historical inquiry and interpretation, and gain an understanding of how important historical events and developments have shaped the modern world. (NCSS, 2018, p. 3)

In Plate IV, the ending of *The Teachings of PtahHotep* (Myer, 1900/2010), the MDW-NTR is very detailed, which Egyptologists attribute to the age of the text. In it, PtahHotep acknowledged that doing the work as vizier:

> has caused me to acquire upon the earth one hundred and ten years of life with the gift of the favor of the king among the first (or, ancients) of those that their works have made noble doing the pleasure of the king in an honored place (i.e., a place of dignity?). It is finished. (Myer, 1900/2010, p. 96)

PtahHotep explains the code of conduct of the ancient Kemites (A. G. Hilliard et al., 1987). This explanation connects with all three NCSS themes: culture, global connection, and time, continuity, and change.

C3 AND *THE TEACHINGS OF PTAHHOTEP*

Using an unbleaching perspective, this chapter applied the C3 Framework in an examination of *The Teachings of PtahHotep* in social studies discourse. Through content analysis of primary source documents, findings indicate that the oldest book in the world has significant implications for social studies discourse and curriculum development particularly as it relates to the C3 Framework. By broadening social studies curriculum development to appeal to diverse learners, this research has the potential to improve professional development for preservice teachers.

Unbleaching the curriculum suggests that counternarratives are important because they underscore the contributions of omitted works like *The Teachings of PtahHotep* (D. Bell, 1980; Crenshaw, 2001; Ladson-Billings, 2003; Ladson-Billings & Tate, 1995). In this regard, unbleaching illustrates how education can be used as an instrument of liberation against systems of oppression and to enhance DEI in education. If the aim of social studies is civic engagement, then providing students with accurate historical accounts is imperative. From an unbleaching perspective, civic competence requires the ability to use knowledge about one's community, nation, and world; apply inquiry processes; and employ skills of data collection and analysis, collaboration, decision making, and problem solving (NCSS, 2018). If access to accurate historical records that include contributions of all of the world's people is minimized, then not only is civic engagement less of a reality, but true education becomes impossible.

Knowledge and understanding of the past enable us to analyze the causes and consequences of events and developments and to place them in the context of the institutions, values, and beliefs of the periods in which they took place (NCSS, 2018). As such, Graness (2016) identifies ancient Egypt as a powerful generator of ideas for Africa and the world and asserts, "It is time to revise the canon of philosophy and to work on a World History of Knowledge and Philosophy, where ancient Egypt will surely have to play an important role" (p. 14). Thus, PtahHotep's book presents old, but also new, insights for education and social studies curriculum development. As unbleaching suggests, it raises questions about power and privilege in education, as well as what counts as knowledge and who is worth studying. In this sense, the social studies curriculum is an effective starting place for curricular change, and unbleaching offers a guiding lens.

As Carter G. Woodson argues in *The Miseducation of the Negro*, failure to teach accurate accounts of human contributions through the reprehensive practice of miseducation and curricular violence is harmful to all learners (Woodson, 1933/2006; Ighodaro & Wiggan, 2011). Per chapter 1, curriculum violence occurs when students experience curricular distortions and omissions and when they see tokenized or distorted representations of themselves, their communities, and their ancestors in the curriculum, which is harmful to both teachers and students (Ighodaro & Wiggan, 2011). Additionally, students become disengaged when they cannot see themselves in the curriculum (J.

E. King & Swartz, 2014; Ladson-Billings, 2009; Obenga & Saakana, 1991). They begin to believe an oppressive master narrative that suggests they are irrelevant (Akbar, 1998; D. Bell, 1995). Given that schools are sites where students experience injurious practices such as "dysconscious racism" and curriculum violence, additional research that addresses curriculum development and instruction is necessary.

Using unbleaching as a lens, the C3 Framework, and original documents from *The Teaching of PtahHotep*, this chapter examines the world's first book and its implications for social studies discourse. The social studies standards themes of culture, global connection, and time, continuity, and change should reflect and include content from the oldest book in the world (Myer, 1900/2010). *The Teachings of PtahHotep* is still available thousands of years after it was recorded, which makes the recommendation to include its maxims in the social studies curriculum and teach about its significance even more important.

Per the unbleaching framework, all students should learn about multicultural contributions to expand their knowledge of the world around them (Banks, 2010; Paris & Alim, 2017; Sleeter & Grant, 1987; Watson-Vandiver & Wiggan, 2018; Wiggan & Watson-Vandiver, 2019b). As unbleaching contends, presenting a comprehensive history of the contributions of all people helps to counteract the negative effects of suppression and exclusion. Similarly, J. E. King and Swartz (2014) advocate for a revised PK–12 curriculum that rigorously analyzes and challenges distortions, disparagements, and erasures and acknowledges and teaches from various epistemological perspectives. NCSS would benefit even more from bringing educators from diverse backgrounds to the table to develop curricula that are centered and culturally inclusive.

Thus, the significance of this discussion is that it unbleaches the curriculum to expand social studies discourse and provides tools that educators can use to introduce *The Teachings of PtahHotep* in classroom instruction. In applying an unbleaching perspective, this research aligns with DEI initiatives. Our findings indicate that including PtahHotep helps to unbleach and broaden social studies curriculum development to appeal to diverse learners. Additionally, the process and practice of unbleaching has the potential to better prepare preservice teachers.

CHAPTER SUMMARY

In sum, this chapter addressed the curricular implications of the world's oldest book. Unbleaching the curriculum to include *The Teachings of PtahHotep* can enhance student learning and inform social studies curriculum development to improve student outcomes. In the next chapter, we explore the curricular implications of the world's oldest mathematical papyrus, the Ahmes Manuscript, for curriculum, instruction, and lesson planning.

Chapter 3

Unbleaching Ancient Equations in Education

The Ahmes Papyrus, the Oldest Mathematical Manuscript

> *Education is for improving the lives of others and for leaving your community and world better than you found them.*
>
> —Marian Wright Edelman

As we have discussed throughout the first two chapters, there are many key issues impacting U.S. public schools including low student performance, an increasingly diverse student population, and a teacher workforce that is 79% White (NCES, 2020). As a result, to improve outcomes as well as processes and practices in education, there remains a need for a curriculum that grounds multicultural perspectives and centers DEI, particularly in science, technology, engineering, and mathematics (STEM) and/or science, technology, engineering, arts, and mathematics (STEAM). Thus, this chapter critically explores how unbleaching the curriculum in STEM can improve student outcomes.

While Egypt's primacy in the development of some of the earliest literature and educational institutions has been documented (Budge, 1920; A. G. Hilliard, 1989; Shaw, 2003; Van de Mieroop, 2021), the unique history of the Ahmes Mathematical Papyrus, the oldest in the world, is misrepresented and largely omitted from the curriculum (Akbar, 1998; Clarke, 1977; Diop, 1974; A. G. Hilliard et al., 1987). Thus, unbleaching is required to create greater inclusion and multicultural perspectives. In this papyrus, Ahmes I (sometimes spelled Ahmose) (ca. 1550–1525 B.C.E.) provides the first known documentation of advanced mathematics. Like PtahHotep who was discussed in the previous chapter, Ahmes I's work is another example of a key omission in the curriculum.

As evidence of bleaching and whitewashing, when Scottish archeologist and antiquarian Alexander Henry Rhind purchased the Ahmes Papyrus in 1858, he renamed it for himself in addition to several other artifacts such as the Rhind Tomb at Sheikh Abd el-Qurna, Thebes (Chace et al., 1929; Rhind, 1862). Hence, the Ahmes Papyrus is often erroneously called the Rhind Manuscript, even though it was written by Ahmes/Ahmose I around 1550 B.C.E. (see Figure 3.1). For the purposes of this work and to maintain historical continuity, the Ahmes Mathematical Papyrus is referred to by its original title (Ahmes Papyrus), rather than the Rhind. At the very least, renaming Indigenous artifacts for Europeans detracts from their historical significance and whitewashes history.

Figure 3.1. Head of Ahmose I, ca. 1550–1525 B.C.E. (Source: Wikimedia Commons)

In addition, defacing artifacts by removal of the nose and lips represents efforts to suppress their Black/African origins (see Figure 3.1). These two practices, renaming and defacing, show how the distortion of history can lead to miseducation, meaning indoctrination and the influence of European thinking under the guise of education, as well as curriculum violence, the deliberate manipulation or misrepresentation of academic programming that compromises the well-being of learners (Ighodaro & Wiggan, 2011; Woodson, 1933/2006).

Dated circa 1550 B.C.E., the Ahmes Papyrus provides a foundation for the development of mathematics. Yet, in spite of its historical significance, it is generally omitted from the curriculum in U.S. public schools (British Museum, n.d.; Chace et al., 1929; Newman, 1952; Sedgwick & Tyler, 1917). This represents the purposeful practice of bleaching to omit, suppress, or falsify non-White contributions and perspectives.

This chapter explores the Ahmes Papyrus (see Figure 3.2) to determine how the process of unbleaching and the inclusion of the world's oldest mathematical papyrus can improve the curriculum, specifically STEM/STEAM and social studies, and create greater DEI. The description of the papyrus, which is currently held in the British Museum (n.d.), indicates:

> Papyrus; Hieratic text verso and recto: the "Rhind Mathematical Papyrus." The papyrus is probably a mathematics textbook, used by scribes to learn to solve particular mathematical problems by writing down appropriate examples. The text includes eighty-four problems with tables of divisions, multiplications, and

Figure 3.2. The Ahmes (Rhind) Papyrus EA10057. (Source: Wikimedia Commons)

handling of fractions; and geometry, including volumes and areas. The scribe, Ahmose, dated the papyrus in year 33 of Apophis, the penultimate king of the Hyksos 15th Dynasty. The other side of the papyrus mentions "year 11" without a king's name, but with a reference to the capture of the city of Heliopolis.

The British Museum (which acquired it in 1865) also indicates that the Ahmes Papyrus was found in Thebes (Upper Egypt) and is dated circa 1550 B.C.E. (British Museum, n.d.). These artifacts confirm the contributions of Ahmes I and the important role he played in the development of mathematics. Thus the need for an unbleached curriculum that includes the contributions of both PtahHotep, whom we discussed in chapter 2, and Ahmes I.

Using the framework of unbleaching, this chapter situates the Ahmes Papyrus in the curriculum by addressing its historical significance and educational implications for teachers, practitioners, and scholars. Applying unbleaching and using case study method, content analysis, and historical detection, this chapter's qualitative research expands DEI discourse. Including critical information such as the Ahmes Papyrus in the curriculum can improve student outcomes and participation in STEM/STEAM careers. Ultimately, this chapter explores multicultural perspectives and curriculum development to address the following guiding question: *What are the educational implications of the Ahmes Papyrus, the oldest mathematical papyrus in the world, for STEM/STEAM and social studies curriculum development?* As such, it is necessary to explore the social and historical context of the Ahmes Papyrus in light of unbleaching.

SOCIAL AND HISTORICAL CONTEXT AND UNBLEACHING

A core part of unbleaching curriculum and instruction, and education in general, is a foundational understanding that all humans are of African descent, as Ethiopia is home to the earliest human fossils, and that all humans share 99.9% of the same DNA (National Human Genome Research Institute, 2006/2011; National Science Foundation [NSF], 2001; Shared DNA, 2005). This means that all of the 8 billion people in the world come from the same family tree and share the same DNA (Shared DNA, 2005; Smedley & Smedley, 2018; United Nations, 2022). In light of these facts, educators must be deliberate in creating lesson plans and curricula that embed DEI and unbleaching practices. Dei (1994) explains the importance of having multiple perspectives in education:

When a teacher gives voice and space to multicentric perspectives and other legitimate interpretations of human experiences, every student in the class, African and non-African, gains from knowing the complete account of events that have shaped human history. (p. 20)

As precursors to Dei's call, scholars such as Joel Augustus Rogers, Carter G. Woodson, W. E. B. Du Bois, Martin R. Delaney, and Alexander Crummell laid a foundation for diversity and inclusion in groundbreaking research that centered African contributions (Wiggan, 2010). In this way, unbleaching seeks to reclaim and uncover suppressed curricular and pedagogical contributions while working for the continued improvement of Africa, the world, and people of African descent, as well as the broader human population and family tree. Additionally, unbleaching aims to create equity and justice for those who have been oppressed based on racialization, social stratification, and cultural domination by the ruling class (Alexander, 2012; G. C. Bell, 2017; Crenshaw et al., 1995; S. D. Dei & Lordan, 2016; Kozol, 2005; Lorde, 1984; Martinez, 2014; Matsuda, 1991; Mertens, 2014).

In the U.S., racial and ethnic relations have been central aspects of the social, economic, and political landscape, and as such, unbleaching provides a framework to analyze these processes and to create change. In this light, unbleaching agitates against and deconstructs Eurocentrism, Whiteness, and hegemonic indoctrination (J. E. King & Swartz, 2014; Wiggan, 2011b). It helps to liberate against hegemony, or cultural dominance of one group over all others, and racialization in schools and society (deMarrais & LeCompte, 1999; Gramsci, 1971). With unbleaching as the guiding framework, the problem of curriculum development in education can be addressed. One key curricular omission is the Ahmes Papyrus (erroneously called the Rhind Mathematical Papyrus), which is at the core of this research.

UNBLEACHING THE CURRICULUM

In light of unbleaching the suppressed contribution of Ahmes, as J. E. King and Swartz (2014) note, "re-membering" history helps to reconnect multiple and shared knowledge bases and experiences of identity groups through conscious inquiry. The authors further explain that "re-membering" history is purposefully designed to reconnect multiple and shared knowledge bases and experiences that shape the past through principles of culturally informed curricular practices and practitioner inquiry.

Regarding Eurocentrism and unbleaching, "re-membering" is appropriate for historical recovery because of the need to broaden the contours and content related to teaching about omissions through accessing and incorporating the ideas and actions of those whose presence and influence are generally on the margins (Asante, 1991; J. E. King & Swartz, 2014, 2015, 2018). In the purview of unbleaching, this is the process of correcting history and the curriculum itself for greater accuracy. In the case of the Ahmes Papyrus, "re-membering" is effective for historical recovery and unbleaching. Teaching students about the contributions of Ahmes I to the field of mathematics is a clear example of how "re-membering" history through curriculum development helps expand students' learning. In the context of education and unbleaching, this is particularly important in regard to impacting the diversity and numbers of students who pursue careers in STEM.

UNBLEACHING: AFRICAN AMERICAN STUDENTS IN STEM

Unbleaching is important in that it helps minority students see themselves in the curriculum, which can influence their STEM/STEAM career choices. Over the next 20 years, jobs in STEM will outpace all other fields (NSF, 2020b). In the U.S., the teacher workforce is 79% White and majority female. However, the student body is 53% minority (NCES, 2018, 2020). Relatedly, according to Ash et al. (2020), in STEM education, 84% of teachers are White. Thus, the profession also needs unbleaching. To advance the U.S. as a global leader in STEM, federal strategic goals aim to expand access to STEM/STEAM education (National Science and Technology Council [NSTC], 2018).

As such, the U.S. will rely heavily on individuals around the world and from different backgrounds to help meet the nation's STEM demands. By extension, this places an enormous responsibility on teacher education and the field of science education in particular. Due to the demand in STEM and the need for STEM/STEAM educators, a growing body of science education research has emerged (Allen & Eisenhart, 2017; Hurtado et al., 2010) with the aim of raising STEM achievement and supporting the entry and persistence of underrepresented minorities in the field (Hurtado et al., 2010; Riegle-Crumb et al., 2011).

Historically, to support racist beliefs about the intellectual capacity and low achievement of minoritized groups, pseudoscience has been positioned in STEM (Ash & Wiggan, 2018; Wiggan, 2007). This is rather problematic, as a Black African named Imhotep is generally regarded as having written the world's first medical manuscript, and as illustrated here, a Black African named Ahmes wrote the oldest mathematical manuscript (Hurry, 1926; Watson-Vandiver & Wiggan, 2018). Nevertheless, through pseudoscience, there have been many attempts to suppress and falsify minority achievements, particularly in STEM. In this light, in contrast to pseudoscience and its racist underpinnings, science refers to "the scholarly and practical discipline concerned with the teaching, learning and assessment of science content, science processes and the nature of science" (McComas, 2014, p. 71). Given the predicted growth of careers in STEM over the next 20 years, a concerted effort to prepare teachers in these areas requires proactive initiatives, as well as an unbleached curriculum that undergirds DEI initiatives (NSF, 2020b).

In light of the effects of COVID-19, STEM research has become even more crucial (Areddy, 2020). The novel coronavirus (SARS-CoV-2) spread quickly, and by March 11, 2020, the World Health Organization (WHO) declared COVID-19 a pandemic (CDC, 2020a, 2020b; WHO, 2020). The subsequent transmission of COVID-19 through global travel and migration has proven to have devastating effects on the global community. Exceeding their capacity and ability to treat overwhelming numbers of patients, health care systems around the world are stretched beyond their limits. Furthermore, the emergence of this global health crisis and its disproportionate impact on Black and Brown communities has left scientists working around the clock to find a cure. As the demand for scientists grows, there are concerns about the preparation of science education candidates, and an overall gap in the supply of teachers in general, which is even more pronounced in STEM (Wiggan et al., 2020). The lack of qualified STEM teachers has had a negative impact on student performance.

STEM IN A NATIONAL AND SOCIAL CONTEXT

According to the National Center for Education Statistics' (2018) "Condition of Education," 40% of U.S. twelfth graders scored below basic proficiency in science, while only 60% demonstrated basic proficiency. With high school preparation being a direct indicator for the STEM labor workforce (Israel, 2017), and with the emergence of a global pandemic, these statistics provide a glaring look into the status of science education and advancement in the U.S. Additionally, based on the number of conferred bachelor's degrees, providing students with the skills they need to be competitive in STEM fields requires an unbleached curriculum that is rigorous and grounded in 21st-century innovation.

According to Fry et al. (2021), data show that females constitute 36% of STEM bachelor's degrees, while males constitute 64%. As of 2018, women earned 85% of the bachelor's degrees in health-related fields, but only 22% in engineering and 19% in computer science (Fry et al., 2021). Relatedly, men earned 15% of degrees in health-related fields. According to the U.S. Census (2021), the U.S. population is 59.3% White (not of Latinx descent), while minorities (non-Whites) constitute 40.7%. However, in 2018, the National Science Foundation reported that Black, Latinx, and Native American workers held only 11% of science and engineering jobs (NSF, 2020c). In this light, the National Association for Multicultural Education contends that the intersections of scientific literacy and diversity and equity are inseparable (National Association for Multicultural Education, 2019). In fact, many multicultural educators suggest that science education must connect to social justice issues and must be culturally responsive to the nation's diverse learners (National Association for Multicultural Education, 2019).

Since U.S. school curricula often overlook or downplay multicultural history, the contribution of minority groups must be highlighted, especially in STEM. Watson-Vandiver and Wiggan (2018) in "The Genius of Imhotep: An Exploration of African-Centered Curricula and Teaching in a High Achieving US Urban School" showed that teachers and students find empowerment through multicultural curriculum and pedagogy. This case study at Barbara Sizemore Academy (BSA, pseudonym), a high-performing African-centered school, explained the perspectives and experiences of students and teachers in a high-achieving minority school. While decentering European hegemony and focusing on the primacy of Africa, BSA centered Black achievers like Ahmes I and Imhotep (Watson-Vandiver & Wiggan, 2018). BSA students benefited from an unbleached curriculum. To this extent, Dei (1994) notes that,

> when a teacher gives voice and space to multicentric perspectives and other legitimate interpretations of human experiences, every student in the class, African and non-African, gains from knowing the complete account of events that have shaped human history. (p. 20)

In this way, from an unbleaching perspective, the curriculum should reflect a comprehensive view of world history from a human-centered perspective rather than a Eurocentric one.

More research is needed to address gaps in the literature regarding DEI in STEM/STEAM. In this chapter, unbleaching guides the analysis of the Ahmes Papyrus and its potential to expand STEM/STEAM discourse through curriculum development. As such, the guiding question for this chapter is: *What are the educational implications of the Ahmes Papyrus, the oldest mathematical papyrus in the world, for STEM/STEAM and social studies curriculum development and education?*

UNBLEACHING AND THE AHMES PAPYRUS

This chapter applies unbleaching to promote human rights and increase social justice in education. As noted in the previous chapter, this research uses case study, content analysis, and historical detection to comprise a tripartite research approach that adds to the rigor and quality of the findings (Krippendorff, 2018; Rhineberger et al., 2005; Yazan, 2015). Methodological triangulation increases the validity of the research. Flick (2002) states, "Triangulation is less a strategy for validating results and procedures than an alternative to validation which increases scope, depth, and consistency in methodological proceedings" (p. 227).

As noted, the tripartite methodology in our work involves case study, content analysis, and historical detection, which are used to analyze primary source documents to address more specifically the question: How can the Ahmes Papyrus (the oldest mathematical document in the world) expand multicultural education to improve student outcomes? Using the framework of unbleaching, this chapter highlights the contributions of the Ahmes Papyrus as the oldest mathematical document (Asante, 1990; Banks, 2010; Gay, 2018; J. E. King & Swartz, 2014; Ladson-Billings & Tate, 1995; NCSS, 2018). The Ahmes Papyrus is the primary sample. As Krippendorff (2018) reveals, content analysis is an empirical research method that promotes reliability, validity, and trustworthiness. This research is strengthened by three triangulated methods—case study, content analysis, and historical detection. Used conjunctively, these add rigor and quality to the study.

As noted above, unbleaching the curriculum helps to correct master-scripted versions of knowledge that perpetuate hegemonic constructions by erroneously recording the past and present. In the parlance of unbleaching, these grand narratives or agreed-upon versions of knowledge are sometimes framed through Eurocentrism, which marginalizes the contributions of Black and Brown people (Loewen, 2008; Swartz, 2013). Swartz (2013) notes:

> Countering the grand narratives that support master scripts can be accomplished by identifying sets of knowledge based on scholarship that locates historically marginalized peoples as subjects and historical agents who speak for and name themselves. (p. 34)

In this way, the Ahmes Papyrus, from an unbleaching perspective, helps to correct the curriculum and create greater accuracy.

A master-scripted curriculum operates within a hierarchy of human worth wherein the dominant group is centered and other groups are marginalized. As noted in chapter 1, since all are part of the same human family tree, an unbleached curriculum emphasizes common humanity where there are multiple perspectives and contributions (Diop, 1967, 1974; Shared DNA, 2005). Therefore, accomplished Africans such as Ahmes I should not be relegated to the margins. An unbleached curriculum does not objectify and emphasize a single group but centers all of humanity. In applying an unbleaching framework, the analysis of the Ahmes Papyrus yields important results.

UNBLEACHING ANCIENT EQUATIONS IN EDUCATION

Within the master-scripted curriculum, there is no mention of the Ahmes Papyrus, as it is only referenced as the Rhind Papyrus. After its purchase in 1858 by Alexander Henry Rhind, the Ahmes Papyrus was renamed and its African origins underrepresented. According to Peet (1923), the Ahmes (now called Rhind) Mathematical Papyrus is housed in the British Museum in two sheets: Papyrus 10057 (319 centimeters length by 33 centimeters height) and Papyrus 10058 (206 centimeters length by 33 centimeters height). Peet (1923) notes:

> The Rhind Papyrus dates from the Hyksos Period, though it claims to be a copy of a document prepared in the XIIth Dynasty, in the reign of Amenemhet III. . . . There is a very definite tendency among Egyptologists to put this period down as the Golden Age of Egyptian knowledge and wisdom. There can be little doubt that some of the literary papyri have their roots in this era, as for example the Proverbs of Ptahhotep, and the antiquated constructions of the medical papyri make it possible that the science of medicine, such as it was, had its spring in the Old Kingdom. (p. 17)

To extend Peet's (1923) analysis, Spalinger (1990) provides a detailed description of the Ahmes Papyrus. However, there is little attribution to its Egyptian origins and more emphasis on the Rhind and the Moscow Papyrus. Spalinger (1990) notes:

> Although the purpose of this study is to present a careful examination of the development of the text—for example, the interrelationships among and between the various problems and their precise position within the text—one healthy by-product of this presentation may be to reawaken an interest in similar papyri, too often ignored in the bulk of Egyptological research. (p. 296)

Spalinger makes a compelling case regarding the significance of the papyri, which is noteworthy. How, then, can students and teachers have no knowledge of Ahmes I, the person who wrote this important manuscript? In short, through whitewashed history (Chace et al., 1929; Peet, 1923; Robins &

Shute, 1987; Spalinger, 1990), renaming, and bleaching, there is suppression and omission regarding the Ahmes Papyrus and its Egyptian origins. From an unbleaching perspective, the historical significance of this document is an important contribution to curriculum development.

As it stands, the importance of mathematical calculations was a factor in constructing the Great Sphinx and the Pyramid of Giza (Gillings, 1972). Similarly, the mysteries of the mathematical calculations needed to construct the Great Sphinx and the Pyramid of Giza are perhaps recorded in the Ahmes Papyrus. The Ahmes Papyrus contains tables for the calculation of area, the conversion of fractions, the structure of elementary sequences, and extensive information about measurement, including division (Danesi, 2018; Peet, 1923; Spalinger, 1990). According to Gillings (1972), the Ahmes Papyrus contains the earliest known symbols for addition, subtraction, and equality. This is an important component of unbleaching the curriculum.

The Rhind (Ahmes) Mathematical Papyrus illustrates the importance of these documents as part of the historical record and an unbleached curriculum. They provide insight into the ancient Egyptians' mathematical genius. From an unbleaching perspective, the Ahmes Papyrus can be highlighted in a curriculum as an example of African contributions to world history. Instead of beginning the story in the middle, rather than at its onset, historians have relegated this important history and largely omitted it (Adichie, 2009). Spalinger (1990) traces the documentation of the Ahmes (Rhind) Papyrus to three primary sources all named *The Rhind Mathematical Papyrus*: Peet (1923), Chace et al. (1929), and Robins-Shute (1987). None of these mention the true Egyptian origins of the document in detail, nor do they reference Ahmes I as much more than a "copyist." In "The Rhind Mathematical Papyrus as a Historical Document," Spalinger (1990) notes:

> The internal history of the treatise, including the later additions, sheds a small yet significant light upon Rhind's development, and its final resting place in Thebes, miles away from its original location, provides an even more intriguing reason why I felt this analysis was necessary. Oddly enough, Rhind does not figure in the worthwhile survey of Cerny, and Caminos' important recent evaluation of reused papyri is ancillary to this study. In essence, Rhind reveals a well-worked development on the part of the copyist, whose careful spacing and beautiful hand provide us today with an excellent exemplar of a first class hieratic document, the value of which is augmented by its excellent state of preservation. (p. 43)

He continues:

> Complete as well, the work has been employed as a basis of palaeography, a study of Egyptian mathematics, and an analysis of Middle Kingdom papyri.

In fact, although dating to the later Hyksos period, and—useful to remember—from lower Egypt, this papyrus reveals its close connection to the Middle Kingdom, as its dimensions overtly testify. But for the purposes of this study, I have deferred any detailed analysis of this aspect of the text, preferring instead to present Rhind as a composite text, and thereby viewing it from a vantage point often considered to be mundane. As a historical document, and just by itself, this mathematical work can stand on its own. Despite or owing to the complicated internal make-up, Rhind is one of the most important hieratic works of Pharaonic Egypt, and it looks back to the days of Dynasty 12 rather than prefiguring those of the next great phase of Egyptian civilization. (p. 43)

As noted here, there is no mention of Ahmes I and his connection to the papyrus. This misinformation compromises the curriculum and leaves learners with the impression that the Ahmes Papyrus did not exist prior to its renaming. Thus, per unbleaching, a historically accurate account of this important mathematical document should begin with acknowledging who Ahmes I was and how this contributes to world history.

EDUCATIONAL IMPLICATION OF THE AHMES PAPYRUS

There are several educational implications of the Ahmes Papyrus, the oldest mathematical papyrus in the world, for STEM, social studies curriculum development, education, and unbleaching the curriculum. The 2018 revision of the NCSS *National Curriculum Standards for Social Studies: A Framework for Teaching, Learning, and Assessment* leaves a noticeable void in the historical record that could potentially contribute to miseducation (Akbar, 1998; NCSS, 2018; Woodson, 1933/2006). Social studies is supposed to provide coordinated, systematic study drawing upon such disciplines as philosophy, religion, sociology, anthropology, archaeology, economics, geography, history, law, political science, and psychology, as well as appropriate content from the humanities, mathematics, and natural sciences (NCSS, 2018). In the U.S., the social studies curriculum currently does not include information about the Ahmes Papyrus. Revisions to the curriculum can address the invisibility of the Ahmes Papyrus in historical documentation and education discourse. The omission of information about the Ahmes Papyrus further suggests that more work is needed to shift from a master-scripted to an unbleached curriculum. Revising the social studies curriculum to include the contributions of the Ahmes Papyrus has the potential to broaden multicultural education to appeal to diverse learners. In this way and from an unbleaching perspective, when history is inclusive with broader social studies knowledge, the presentation of the past is connected to our own possibilities for action in the present (Swartz, 2013). Including critical information such as the Ahmes Papyrus in the curriculum can improve student outcomes for marginalized youth, especially as it pertains to participation in STEM careers.

In the purview of unbleaching, a hegemonic curriculum represents harmful practice because it devalues students' identity by omitting or including tokenized representations. In the purview of education, when students are the beneficiaries of a corrected curriculum that is accurate and relevant, their prospects for academic success are improved. Multiple studies show that high achievement is more likely when the curriculum is inclusive (Chenoweth & Theokas, 2013; Watson-Vandiver & Wiggan, 2020; Wiggan & Watson-Vandiver, 2019a). Access to a quality education is the foundation of a democratic society and characteristic of a productive nation. Thus, there is a need for more research that investigates multicultural perspectives through unbleaching the curriculum—to promote DEI in education processes and practices.

CHAPTER SUMMARY

Applying the unbleaching framework to the Ahmes Papyrus, the oldest mathematical manuscript, this chapter addressed its educational implications within STEM, curriculum development, and education. In the next chapter, we explore the contributions of Imhotep, the Father of Medicine, within the context of an unbleached curriculum.

Chapter 4

"He Look Like Tupac!"
Imhotep, the Father of Medicine

> *I have never encountered any children in any group who are not geniuses. There is no mystery on how to teach them. The first thing you do is treat them like human beings and the second thing you do is love them.*
>
> —*Asa G. Hilliard*

In the previous chapter, we discussed the Ahmes Manuscript, which as the preponderance of the evidence suggests is the oldest mathematical manuscript, subsequently renamed the Rhind Manuscript in 1862 for Scottish antiquarian Alexander Rhind (Chace et al., 1929; Rhind, 1862). To date, there is less knowledge about the manuscript and its connection to Ahmes, STEM/STEAM, and U.S. public schools, which would align it with the *Framework for K–12 Science Education* (National Research Council, 2012) and the National Science Foundation's *STEM Education for the Future: 2020 Visioning Report* (NSF, 2020c). Much like Ahmes, there is less knowledge about Imhotep. As such, this chapter explores Imhotep and his contributions as the Father of Medicine (Osler, 1913/1921; Peltier, 1990; Pinch, 2002). It explores an unbleached and corrected curriculum that centers Imhotep in STEM/STEAM, as well as in curriculum and instruction to promote greater DEI.

In the quest for equitable practices and greater inclusion for students, particularly those interested in STEM/STEAM careers, curriculum reform can bring about equity and excellence in education for all (A. G. Hilliard & Sizemore, 1984; Ladson-Billings, 2009; Watson-Vandiver & Wiggan, 2018; Wiggan, 2008). To this end, an unbleached curriculum is a crucial aspect of correcting and repositioning education as a source of liberation against oppressive systems of exclusion (Freire, 1970/2018; hooks, 2014).

As discussed in the previous chapters, curricular omissions and suppressed contributions such as *The Teachings of PtahHotep* and the Ahmes Papyrus are embedded in an educational system that has been bleached and whitewashed. Thus, unbleaching can situate these contributions in a curriculum that promotes DEI and right knowledge—meaning interrogating all claims of facts, including pseudoscience, to reveal greater truth (Watson-Vandiver & Wiggan, 2021). Given the state of U.S. public schools, the national underperformance and underrepresentation of minorities in STEM/STEAM, and multiple curricular omissions including the contributions of Imhotep, the Father of Medicine, there is a need to *correct* the curriculum to emphasize DEI and incorporate more social justice processes and practices (Hurry, 1926; Osler, 1913/1921; Peltier, 1990; Pinch, 2002). Much like general education, the STEM/STEAM curriculum has been whitened up so that notable contributions like Imhotep's are omitted in order to tell a single story (Adichie, 2009) that reflects a limited Europeanized or whitewashed perspective.

Additionally, in the purview of achievement, U.S. public schools reflect underperformance in STEM across the country (NCES, 2020; National Research Council, 2012). These data are discussed in greater detail later in the chapter. Compounding these issues is the fact that the public school teacher workforce is 79% White, while more than 53% of students are minorities (NCES, 2020). An increasingly diverse public school population indicates that minority students are now the majority. As a result, there is a need to better prepare teacher educators to unbleach and correct the curriculum to address DEI and include multiple perspectives.

Per NCSS, to develop the tools needed to engage "civic competence" and become global citizens, all students can benefit from DEI and multicultural perspectives in the curriculum (Banks, 2010; NCSS, 2018; Tatum, 2007). This is not just beneficial for Black and Brown or other minority students; it is helpful for all learners. As noted previously, unbleaching is a purposeful process intended to dismantle systems of racial oppression, as well as falsification and omission surrounding minoritized people's contributions and perspectives. Thus, to disrupt systems of oppression that maintain power and privilege, this chapter highlights an important aspect of an unbleached curriculum—the contributions of Imhotep, the Father of Medicine (Hurry, 1926; Osler, 1913/1921; Peltier, 1990; Pinch, 2002; Watson-Vandiver & Wiggan, 2018). To this point, the Centre for Biomedical Egyptology explains that Egyptian doctors were practicing credible medicine for over a millennium before the Greek physician Hippocrates was born (A. G. Hilliard, 1989; Serageldin, 2013).

Imhotep, whom the Greeks also called Asclepius (also spelled Asclepius/Asclepios/Askelepios), "the Father of Medicine," was a Black Egyptian who is honored in the Hippocratic oath (discussed later in the chapter), which is still recited by medical doctors as they graduate and are inducted into the field (Garrett, 1978; Osler, 1913/1921; Peltier, 1990; Pinch, 2002). To the point regarding the importance of Imhotep in STEM and the field of medicine in particular, Breasted (1930) explains:

> In the history of medical science in particular, it was no accident that the leading patron god of medicine in early classical Europe [Imhotep] who was called Asclepios by the Greeks and Aesculapius by the Romans was originally an historical personage, an ancient Egyptian wise man and physician called Imhotep by the Egyptians, grand vizier, chief architect, and royal medical advisor of the Pharaoh in the Thirtieth Century [B.C.E.], the earliest known physician in history. (p. 3)

As Breasted (1930) suggests, Imhotep was the person the Greeks and Romans regarded as the pioneer in the field of medicine. In this sense, modern medicine owes its genesis to an African vizier, multi-genius, and physician named Imhotep (Breasted, 1930; Brandt-Rauf & Brandt-Rauf, 1987; *British Medical Journal*, 1927; Garrett, 1978; Hurry, 1926; Risse, 1986; Sprunt, 1955). Nonetheless, Hippocrates, who lived between 460 B.C.E. and 370 B.C.E., is generally heralded as the presumed Father of Medicine (Potter & Smith, 1923). However, Imhotep, who lived at least 1,000 years before Hippocrates, was a master scientist and the chief architect of the Step Pyramid at Saqqara under King Djoser, ruler of ancient Egypt (originally named Kemet) during the Third Dynasty (between 2980 B.C.E. and 2650 B.C.E.), and he was also a physician (Asante, 2000; Brandt-Rauf & Brandt-Rauf, 1987; Diop, 1981b; Hurry, 1926; Osler, 1913/1921). According to Osler (1913/1921), Imhotep is "the first figure of a physician to stand out clearly from the mists of antiquity" (para. 34). In fact, even the Greeks referred to Imhotep (also known as Asclepius/Asclepios/Askelepios) as the god of medicine (Osler, 1913/1921; Peltier, 1990; Pinch, 2002).

Imhotep, PtahHotep, Ahmes, and other pervasive omissions from the NCSS standard course of study and the purposeful whitewashing of history perpetuate miseducation and curriculum violence (Ighodaro & Wiggan, 2011). Using the unbleaching framework, this chapter explores the contributions of Imhotep and the implications for STEM/STEAM and curriculum development as a mechanism to counter miseducation. Thus, the guiding research question for this chapter is: *What are the educational implications of Imhotep, the Father of Medicine, for STEM/STEAM and an unbleached curriculum?* A noticeable gap exists as it pertains to the curriculum, STEM/STEAM, and minority contributions. Through a greater focus on DEI and by educating students about the contributions of Imhotep, there is the potential

Figure 4.1. Imhotep, Father of Medicine. (Source: Authors)

to promote greater engagement in STEM/STEAM, as well as to improve U.S. student achievement and outcomes.

Below we discuss an urban school presentation and workshop we conducted that explored minority contributions in the curriculum. In introducing Imhotep and sharing an image of him from the Imhotep Museum in Egypt, one of the students shouted out, "He look like Tupac!" There was a moment of silence, and then many students commented, "Yeah, it do." In that moment, the students were able to make a connection between Tupac, a contemporary cultural icon, and Imhotep, an ancient African philosopher and scientist. Per the student's comment, phenotypically, Imhotep had distinct African or Black features, as Tupac did.

Part 1 of this chapter makes the connections between the student's comment, "He look like Tupac!" as well as the life of Tupac, and Imhotep as DEI issues. Part 2 discusses Imhotep as the Father of Medicine and explains the implications of his work for unbleaching the curriculum and promoting DEI in STEM/STEAM.

PART 1: UNBLEACHING AND MUSIC AS LIBERATING LITERATURE

Upon seeing an image of Imhotep, "the Father of Medicine," for the very first time, a high school student made an immediate connection, noting, "He look like Tupac!" Exploring the similarities in the phenotype of Tupac and Imhotep based on skin color and physical features provided an opportunity to discuss how these two multi-geniuses are connected in other ways. Thus, the statement "He look like Tupac!" is the impetus for this chapter and reflects the need to connect the past and present to incorporate the contributions of a modern cultural icon, Tupac Shakur (also known as Tupac, 2Pac, and Makaveli) and Imhotep, an Egyptian multi-genius, who may both be particularly relevant in promoting greater DEI in curriculum development (Dyson, 2006; Garrett, 1978; Grimes, 2014; Risse, 1986).

Beyond phenotype, Tupac and Imhotep share some similarities. Like Imhotep, Tupac was a major thinker and leader (Dyson, 2006; Stanford, 2011). Born in 1971 in Harlem, New York, Tupac gained world renown as a rapper, actor, and activist. As a philosopher, an icon of hip-hop culture, and a social justice change agent, Tupac advocated against White supremacy and discrimination and, in a tangential way, supported the principles of unbleaching and the need for social justice in education (Akom, 2009; Dyson, 2006; M. L. Hill, 2009; McKenna, 2015). With songs like "Keep Ya Head Up," "Dear Mama," "Black Cotton," and numerous others, Tupac revolutionized popular culture by helping to change the thinking of listeners through socially conscious lyrics that challenged the status quo (Dyson, 2006; Grimes, 2014; Stanford, 2011). While Tupac does have commercial songs that are less conscious, below we purposefully use examples from ones that are focused on social justice.

Like Imhotep, Tupac would be considered a multi-genius. In the case of Tupac, he used music as a liberating tool to counter the hegemony, bleaching, and whitewashing that center Eurocentric perspectives as the dominant narrative. Tupac's accomplishments as a philosopher, musician, actor, and social thinker were driven by his commitment to social justice (Grimes, 2014). Stanford (2011) explains that, as a cultural worker, Tupac utilized the culture of young people living in urban areas who had come of age during the 1990s as an organizing tool for community and political activity. As we discuss in Part 2 of this chapter, in a similar way, Imhotep had a profound impact on his

Figure 4.2. Tupac Shakur. (Source: 2PAC, 2PAC png)

community and country (Sprunt, 1955). Prior to his untimely assassination, in an interview Tupac explained his motivation:

> The concept behind this [Tupac's Underground Railroad Group] is the same concept behind Harriet Tubman, to get my brothers who might be into drug dealing or whatever it is that's illegal or who are disenfranchised by today's society—I want to get them back by turning them onto music. It could be R&B, hip hop or pop, as long as I can get them involved. While I'm doing that, I'm teaching them to find a love for themselves so they can love others and do the same thing we did for them to others. (Davey D., 1991, interview transcript)

In the role of political advocate, educator, and motivator, Tupac was critically important to the hip-hop community and urban youth as an activist who used music as liberation literature or as a way to help free the minds of the oppressed from oppressive social systems.

According to Hamilton (1993), liberation literature is a pathway to spiritual freedom through consciousness raising. This might explain why in a curriculum and DEI workshop in a local high school, on seeing an image of Imhotep, a student commented, "He look like Tupac!" While simultaneously issuing a call to action, Tupac raised consciousness about social issues and injustices through liberation literature, a body of work that transcends the boundaries of trials, suffering, and triumph (T. O. Jackson & Boutte, 2009). For example, in the song "Keep Ya Head Up," Tupac, the master poet, brought attention to the plight of women in U.S. society (Dyson, 2006). In addition to paying tribute to impoverished Black women who have experienced difficulties, he calls for healing and support. This song highlights the challenges people from low socioeconomic levels encounter in everyday life. Here Tupac notes that all humans originated from a woman known as Lucy (also called Dinkinesh), whose 4-million-year-old remains were discovered in Ethiopia, which is the only uncolonized African country in the world (Wiggan, 2015; Wynn et al., 2021).

As we noted, Ethiopia, a Greek word that means "burnt of skin," is the cradle of the human family tree (Budge 1928/2015). This theme of advocacy for women and consciousness raising is a part of Tupac's body of work. Similarly, "Dear Mama" is an anthem of love written by Tupac to his mother, Afeni Shakur Davis, for the challenges she faced raising him in a major urban city center with threats of economic insecurity, political unrest, gang violence, and a drug epidemic (Dyson, 2006; Guy, 2010; Shakur et al., 2003). Calling her a Black queen, Tupac honors his mother who was a member of the Black Panther Party for Self-Defense (Dyson, 2006). He acknowledges the challenges his mother faced raising him as a Black boy and lets her know he understands her trials and appreciates her.

Tupac's capacity for positivity in his music and its message helped to raise consciousness about social justice issues in the communities he grew up in as well as in world audiences. In our curriculum and DEI workshop, this was perhaps another theme the young man saw that made him make a connection between Tupac and Imhotep. In the case of the former, his reach surpassed the borders of the U.S. and led to international stardom even posthumously. His song "Black Cotton" reminded listeners of the need for addressing oppression and injustices in society. In "Black Cotton," Tupac makes the connection to the cotton that formerly enslaved African people picked to enrich America, and the Black cotton or "slavery" in the modern era that represents the prison-industrial complex (Davis, 2000; Love, 2019; Wilder, 2013). He views Black cotton as a symbol of unrewarded struggle, and the need to redress and mitigate for reparations.

In this way, Tupac's message to future generations is that times have changed, but systems have not. Toward this end, the bleaching that occurs in the curriculum and in education is a significant part of those systems of oppression. Considered one of the most influential artists of all time, Tupac will long be remembered as a modern cultural icon and multi-genius. His contributions to music as an instrument of liberation continue to have an impact on the world. Perhaps to this point, the student in our workshop, after viewing an image of Imhotep, noted, "He look like Tupac!" Below, in Part

2 of this chapter, we discuss Imhotep and his contributions and curricular implications.

PART 2: IMHOTEP: THE FATHER OF MEDICINE

As a precursor of Tupac, Imhotep (who lived between 2980 B.C.E. and 2650 B.C.E.), was a multi-genius and scholar who was held in high regard among Egyptians, Romans, and the Greeks. As this chapter explains, in the parlance of DEI, STEM/STEAM, and curriculum development, the inclusion of Imhotep, the Father of Medicine, has great implications for expanding the curriculum and increasing student achievement (Hurry, 1926; Osler, 1913/1921; Peltier, 1990; Pinch, 2002). From our high school workshop, the point here is that the students were able to make a connection between the phenotype of Tupac, whom they knew of, and Imhotep, whom most students had never seen or heard of. The paradox is that Imhotep, an African or Black person, is the Father of Medicine, yet most of these students from a majority-Black urban school had never heard of him. We further examine the contributions of Imhotep below. Per the unbleaching framework, the knowledge of Imhotep's work and its inclusion in a corrected curriculum is not just for minority students; it is for all students.

UNBLEACHING THE CURRICULUM AND IMHOTEP

Perhaps the reason Imhotep is less known is that his actual manuscript was renamed or whitened up to bear the name of Edwin Smith, an antiquities dealer who in 1862 renamed the Imhotep Papyrus the "Edwin Smith Papyrus" (Chace et al., 1929; Meltzer & Sanchez, 2014; Rhind, 1862). The issue of power and privilege and renaming Indigenous people and artifacts is a theme throughout European enslavement, colonization, and modern history. In an attempt to whiten up history, like the Ahmes Papyrus which we discussed in the previous chapter, the works of Imhotep have been co-opted and generally misrepresented in history, which perhaps is a clear indication of a need for unbleaching (Aldridge, 2014; Asante, 2000; Brandt-Rauf & Brandt-Rauf, 1987; Diop, 1981a; Hurry, 1926; Osler, 1913/1921; Serageldin, 2013). Nonetheless, much like Tupac's songs, Imhotep's contributions have been preserved in monuments such as the one shown in Figure 4.3, which speaks to his influence in Egypt and beyond.

Again, the student in our workshop who commented, "He look like Tupac!" suggests the connection between Imhotep and Tupac in the similarity of their appearances as men with Black phenotypes. As noted previously, the

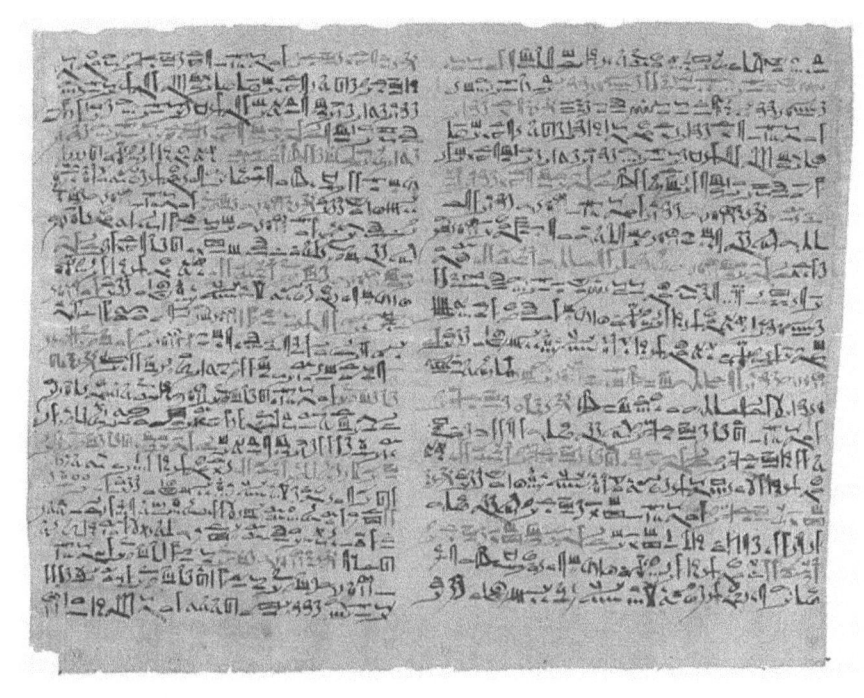

Figure 4.3. Imhotep Papyrus, renamed the Edwin Smith Papyrus in 1862. (Source: Wikimedia Commons)

medical papyrus Imhotep wrote no longer bears his name. Unfortunately, it was renamed by the person who purchased it (Breasted, 1930). The Imhotep Papyrus (now called the Edwin Smith Papyrus) is the oldest known medical treatise; it contains the earliest-known scientific writings on rational observations in medicine (Breasted, 1930). Written in the 16th century B.C.E., it contains approximately 48 medical cases including diagnosis and treatment (see Figure 4.3 for plates from the manuscript).

The original Imhotep Papyrus was found in a tomb in Thebes, Egypt, and sold to antiquities dealer Edwin Smith (Breasted, 1930). Since Smith was not a medical doctor capable of writing such a comprehensive work, he also could not translate it (Breasted, 1930; van Middendorp et al., 2010). As evidence of bleaching and whitewashing, Smith renamed the papyrus in honor of himself. In 1906, it was donated to the New York Historical Society and later translated by Egyptologist James Henry Breasted with the assistance of physician Arno Luckhardt (Breasted, 1930; van Middendorp et al., 2010).

According to Breasted (1930), the original Imhotep Papyrus was written circa the 16th century B.C.E. However, the hieroglyphics or MDW-NTR (pronounced "meh-doo neh-ter") suggest it could have been written around 3000–2500 B.C.E. Imhotep who served under the Third Dynasty of Pharaoh

Djoser (26th century B.C.E.) is asserted as the author of the oldest known medical papyrus (Breasted, 1930). Describing the author of the world's oldest medical document, Breasted (1930) notes:

> The author of our treatise was one of a group of men who will . . . inevitably have been children of their time. We cannot conceive that they ever ceased to believe in the power of magic; but they had learned that in surgery and medicine they were confronted by a great body of observable phenomena, which they systematically and scientifically collected, sometimes out of interest in the salvation of the patient, sometimes out of pure interest in the scientific truth. The class of men thus revealed to us are the earliest natural scientists of whom we know anything, who, confronting a world of objective phenomena, made and organized their observations and based inductive conclusions upon bodies of observed fact. (p. 15)

Breasted's (1930) observations suggest a respect for the validity of the Imhotep Papyrus and a disregard for or oversight of the author in popular literature, with sometimes no direct acknowledgment of Imhotep as the actual author.

However, according to the Centre for Biomedical Egyptology, over 1,000 years before Hippocrates was born, Egyptian doctors were practicing credible medicine (Serageldin, 2013). In noting, "He look like Tupac!" our students in an urban high school made a connection in their minds that Imhotep looks like Tupac, who also looks like them. As a benefit to all students, not just Black students, a corrected curriculum based on DEI principles should incorporate Imhotep as the Father of Medicine and his manuscript (Hurry, 1926; Osler, 1913/1921; Peltier, 1990; Pinch, 2002). This could serve as a great starting place for STEM education (Ash et al., 2020; Gay, 2018; Watson-Vandiver & Wiggan, 2018). The book *Teacher Education to Enhance Diversity in STEM* (Ash et al., 2020) makes a compelling case for DEI work in the field of STEM and provides strategies and resources for teachers. As an example of this needed work, the implications and significance of Imhotep and his work are discussed below.

The Imhotep Papyrus is a medical textbook on trauma surgery that contains detailed medical information including the first descriptions of cranial sutures, the meninges, the external surface of the brain, cerebrospinal fluid, and intracranial pulsations, as well as diagnoses and treatments for multiple injuries. The advances in Egyptian knowledge regarding medical practices far surpassed the Greeks' understanding. The Edwin Smith Surgical Papyrus (Breasted, 1930) confirms the importance of Imhotep's work among the Greeks. He explains:

> In the history of medical science in particular, it was no accident that the leading patron god of medicine in early classical Europe—he [Imhotep] who was called Aesculapius by the Romans—was originally an historical personage, an ancient Egyptian wise man and physician called Imhotep by the Egyptians, grand vizier, chief architect, and royal medical advisor of the Pharaoh in the Thirtieth Century [B.C.E.], the earliest known physician in history. (p. 3)

Imhotep's contributions, however, have been whitened up in the historical record to the extent that his name is hardly associated with the actual manuscript. Instead, his work is now known as the Edwin Smith Papyrus, and Hippocrates is often heralded as the Father of Medicine (Brandt-Rauf & Brandt-Rauf, 1987). However, Greek rulers of Egypt referred to Imhotep as Asclepius (also spelled Aesculapius), a healing god. Hippocrates's *Aphorisms* (Scholtz, 1941) contains the Hippocratic oath, which pays homage to Imhotep (Asclepius) as follows:

> I swear by Apollo the physician, and Asclepius, and Hygieia and Panacea and all the gods and goddesses as my witnesses, that, according to my ability and judgement, I will keep this Oath and this contract. (U.S. National Library of Medicine, 2012)

Today, all medical doctors take this oath, and the contributions of Imhotep are veiled in this Greco-Roman adaptation of his name with a somewhat limited understanding of Imhotep's broader significance. Symptomatic of bleaching and whitewashing, this practice of renaming known artifacts frequently occurs in public school curricula, thus requiring a DEI response to promote social justice and equity in education. Moreover, the practice of renaming reinforces the need for an unbleached curriculum that reflects multiple perspectives in STEM/STEAM.

According to the National Science Foundation, over the next 20 years, jobs in STEM fields will outpace jobs in all other fields (NSF, 2020b). Because of the underperformance of students in STEM preparation, the future standing of the U.S. in the global economy has been a concern (LaForce et al., 2016). According to the Trends in International Mathematics and Science Study (TIMSS, 2019), on a scale of 0 to 1,000, the average fourth-grade mathematics score was about 560 for the U.S. And in eighth-grade mathematics, the average score was 520 (TIMSS, 2019). These were rather modest performances, and clearly much work is needed to improve STEM outcomes.

The TIMSS performance may suggest that a corrected and improved curriculum could enhance student achievement and DEI in U.S. schools. When students can connect to the content they are learning, as evident in the comment "He look like Tupac!", their levels of engagement and performance can be enhanced (Ladson-Billings, 2009; Watson-Vandiver & Wiggan, 2021).

This also means that there is great potential for implementing a multicultural STEM/STEAM curriculum (Ash et al., 2020; NSTC, 2018). The data highlight U.S. school performance in STEM/STEAM and the need for reform. As such, expanding and increasing the quality and rigor of the curriculum may benefit all students.

U.S. underperformance in STEM is also reflected in low science scores. In fourth-grade and eighth-grade science, the average score was approximately 550 on a scale of 0 to 1,000 (TIMSS, 2019). This modest performance may suggest that there is an opportunity to close the equity gaps in mathematics and science in U.S. public schools. With an unbleached curriculum that includes multicultural perspectives and contributions of scientists like Imhotep and Ahmes, whom we discussed in the previous chapter, there is an opportunity to expand the educational outcomes of all learners.

Given the general U.S. underperformance, there is a need to prepare students with 21st-century technology skills for STEM/STEAM careers. Additionally, a corrected curriculum that includes the contributions of Imhotep presents an expanded approach to K–12 science education that could help engage students and address ongoing underperformance. As a national standard and benchmark, in 2012, *A Framework for K–12 Science Education* (National Research Council, 2012) identified eight essential elements of a complete K–12 science and engineering curriculum: (1) personalization of learning; (2) problem-based learning; (3) rigorous learning; (4) career, technology, and life skills; (5) school community and belonging; (6) external community; (7) staff foundations; and (8) external factors. LaForce et al. (2016) identified several key components of this in STEM schools: (1) problem-based learning; (2) rigorous learning; (3) personalization of learning—core instructional; (4) career, technology, and life skills; (5) school community and belonging—core noninstructional; (6) external community—core noninstructional; (7) staff foundations supporting; and (8) essential factors supporting. Providing the foundation for the Next Generation Science Standards (NGSS), these technological tools aid in the understanding of mathematical concepts as well as core concepts in the field of science.

A later publication, Dynamic Learning Maps (2019), offers strategies for teaching science at the elementary, middle, and high school levels, and perhaps provides space and context where the contributions of Imhotep can help unbleach the curriculum and disrupt whitewashing. Similarly, as noted in the National Science Foundation's *STEM Education for the Future: 2020 Visioning Report* (NSF, 2020c):

> All citizens can contribute to our nation's progress and vibrancy. To be prepared for the STEM careers of the future, all learners must have an equitable opportunity to acquire foundational STEM knowledge. The STEM Education of the

Future brings together our advanced understanding of how people learn with modern technology to create more personalized learning experiences, to inspire learning, and to foster creativity from an early age. It will unleash and harness the curiosity of young people and adult learners across the United States, cultivating a culture of innovation and inquiry, and ensuring our nation remains the global leader in science and technology discovery and competitiveness. (p. 5)

Achieving this level of innovation and inquiry means developing creative strategies for the STEM classroom, including lesson plans in which the contents of the Imhotep Papyrus can be infused. This can add interest to the science curriculum by introducing students to Imhotep's contributions as they pertain to illustrating the organization and interaction of major organs into systems in the body. Since the Imhotep Papyrus contains approximately 48 medical cases including diagnosis and treatment, there is potential for student engagement (Breasted, 1930; Brandt-Rauf & Brandt-Rauf, 1987; *British Medical Journal*, 1927; Garrett, 1978; Hurry, 1926; Risse, 1986; Sprunt, 1955).

As when the student in our workshop noted, "He look like Tupac!" the benefits for multicultural and culturally responsive STEM education can help to engage students. As such, the unbleaching framework provides a process for countering miseducation and mitigating curriculum violence (Ighodaro & Wiggan, 2011; Woodson, 1933/2006). Much like Imhotep, as a multi-genius and philosopher, Tupac Shakur helped to raise social awareness and expand the minds of millions of people with socially conscious music that helped promote healing.

Similarly, the contributions of Imhotep and the importance of the Imhotep Papyrus are crucial components of an unbleached curriculum that grounds DEI as well as disrupts silence, exclusionary practices, and falsifications in the interests of White supremacy. This is wrong and must be corrected. Given that U.S. public schools have at least 53% minority students, and that number is expected to increase even more over the next two decades, and the teacher force remains majority White, the need for unbleaching is pressing. Thus, in light of these data, the importance of teacher preparation programs that emphasize multicultural perspectives is critical for all students (Banks, 2010; Gay, 2018; Ladson-Billings, 2009).

As we argue, an unbleached curriculum can help create greater DEI and promote student interest in STEM careers. In the purview of unbleaching and the student who commented, "He look like Tupac!" these words might be a reminder for us all about the power of inclusion and the extent to which right knowledge has been suppressed to promote White supremacy thinking. As Joyce King reminds us, racism can be conscious or dysconscious, and as such, the curriculum must become a central place for redesign (J. E. King,

2015). In this sense, unbleaching helps to promote right knowledge, healing, and wellness not just for minority students, teachers, and administrators, but for all (Ash et al., 2020; Gay, 2018; Watson-Vandiver & Wiggan, 2021).

CHAPTER SUMMARY

In this chapter, we applied the unbleaching framework and explored the contributions of Imhotep and his connection to STEM. As we noted, in an urban high school presentation on DEI in the curriculum, upon seeing an image of Imhotep, a student commented, "He look like Tupac!" This comment spoke to the rest of the group as the students responded, "Yeah, it do." The phenotypical connections the students saw opened the door wide through an expanded, corrected curriculum. "He look like Tupac!" provided a space for culturally responsive teaching, and to disrupt curriculum violence. Given the U.S. national underperformance in STEM, as illustrated in the data presented in this chapter, the public school curriculum can benefit from unbleaching and greater DEI work. It is interesting that the person who is generally credited with starting the field of medicine is not even mentioned in the public school curriculum and is lesser known in education in general, and STEM/STEAM in particular. Given Imhotep's role as the Father of Medicine and the author of the oldest medical papyrus, his contributions are crucial for an unbleached curriculum that promotes multicultural perspectives and DEI processes and practices (Banks, 2010; Osler, 1913/1921; Peltier, 1990; Pinch, 2002). As a continuation of the need for a corrected curriculum, the next chapter provides an analysis of the contributions of the Olmec, the oldest civilization in the Americas.

Chapter 5

The Olmec

Ancient Civilizations in the Americas

> *Intellectuals ought to study the past not for the pleasure they find in so doing, but to derive lessons from it.*
>
> —Cheikh Anta Diop

Connecting to the previous chapter which addressed Imhotep, the Father of Medicine, this chapter seeks to uncover the contributions of ancient civilizations in the Americas. This chapter presents the Olmec's (800 B.C.E.) entry into the region and their impact on civilization. It provides a counternarrative to the master script that positions Christopher Columbus as the "discoverer" of the "New World" and highlights the pre-Columbus presence of the Olmec, the oldest civilization in America (Clarke, 1979; Kubal, 2008; Thatcher, 1903). It explores the educational implications of the Olmec for teachers and social studies curriculum development. Olmec contributions to Mesoamerican history can expand educational discourse. The findings indicate that the Olmec pioneered the first city in the Americas—La Venta, Mexico, also called Olmec City—and as such, they are crucial to the history of the Americas and multicultural curriculum development (Coe et al., 2019; Diehl, 2001, 2004; Van Sertima, 1976/2003). Hence, the Olmec upends the Columbus "discovery myth" and should be centrally placed in the curriculum, as they are the true pioneers of the region. They are a proper starting point in the treatise on the Americas in a corrected curriculum.

Ultimately, this chapter aims to help unbleach the curriculum to reflect the Olmec contributions and address falsifications, omissions, and suppressions. Thus, the guiding question in this chapter is: *What are the educational implications of the Olmec, the oldest civilization in America, for unbleaching the curriculum and enhancing student learning?* First, the chapter explains the role of the Olmec and their early civilization in the Americas. Then it addresses why unbleaching is necessary for correcting whitewashing and promoting DEI in education processes and practices to improve student outcomes.

Matthew Stirling's 1945 National Geographic Society–Smithsonian Institution's archaeological excavation of colossal heads with distinctly non-European features in San Lorenzo and Veracruz, Mexico provides compelling evidence regarding the presence of Olmec in the Americas (Smithsonian Archives, n.d.; Stirling, 1943, 1955). The Olmec presence dates back to circa 800 B.C.E. or earlier, prior to Columbus's arrival in 1492 (Coe et al., 2019; Diehl, 2004; Grove, 2014; Stirling, 1955; Van Sertima, 1976/2003; Weircinski, 1972). While many debate the racial and ethnic identity of the Olmec, readers can determine that for themselves. However, the point here is that the Olmec have been excluded from the curriculum, and they should be centrally positioned at the beginning as opposed to the Columbus discovery myth.

In the case of Mexico, in 1862, a rancher found a large basalt head near Tres Zapotes. José María Melgar y Serrano (1869a, 1869b, 1871) named it the colossal head of Hueyapan, sketched it, and published an article in *Seminario Ilustrado*, where he notes:

> As a work of art it is without exaggeration a magnificent sculpture as may be judged by the photograph which accompanies this. But what amazed me most was the Ethiopian type which it represented. (Melgar y Seranno quoted in Stirling, 1943, p. 17)

Per Melgar y Serrano's (1869c) suggestion, the "Ethiopian" (which is a Greek word meaning "burnt of skin" or "Black") features he noted, with a broad nose and full lips, are in his view Black profile features. Stirling (1943) notes that Melgar y Serrano (1871) attempted to "prove the former existence of a Negro population in Middle America" (Stirling, 1943, p. 17). Again, the point of this chapter is not the race of the Olmec but the fact that their arrival in the Americas predates Columbus, and yet they are hardly mentioned in the curriculum and are generally not known by most educators or curriculum designers. While many are still debating the race of the Olmec, that is not the contribution. Rather, their inclusion in the curriculum is the bigger issue. Readers can view the busts and other artifacts and decipher the Olmec phenotype for themselves.

Per Melgar y Serrano's (1869b) suggestion, the first Olmec colossal head at Hueyapan, and subsequently, the 16 other Olmec colossal heads' profiles appear to be phenotypically Black (Melgar y Serrano, 1869b, 1871; Stirling, 1943, 1955; Van Sertima, 1976/2003; Wicke, 1965). Similarly, Figure 5.1

Figure 5.1. Olmec Colossal Head Discovery at San Lorenzo Monument 1. (Source: Wikicommons)

shows Matthew Stirling's excavation of "El Rey," called the King because of its enormous size and stature (Stirling, 1955). Other members of the archaeological expedition standing next to El Rey show the massiveness of this colossal head, which was carved from basalt (Stirling, 1955).

Archaeological findings reveal over 16 distinctly non-European or "Negroid" colossal heads (as Stirling [1955] reports), step pyramids resembling those found in Ethiopia, Kush (Sudan), ancient Kemet (Egypt), and Niger, as well as developed hieroglyphic writing systems, including a calendar (Barton, 2001; Coe et al., 2019; Diehl, 2004; Stirling, 1955; Van Sertima, 1976/2003; Weircinski, 1972).

In fact, one stone head is even named "El Negro" (meaning "the Black") at the Tuxteco Regional Museum in Mexico (Tuxteco Regional Museum, n.d.). While some researchers (Haslip-Viera et al., 1997) note that the word "Negro" could mean a darker Indigenous person or someone with a painted face, again there is some documentation that non-Europeans or Blacks sailed to this region before Columbus (Van Sertima, 1976/2003; Vaughn, 1998). It is therefore plausible that the Black features Stirling and others noted are vestiges left of their presence, which was also suggested by findings from the Smithsonian Institution (Smithsonian National Museum of Natural History, n.d.; Ubelaker & Angel, 1974). The Olmec are a glaring omission and/or suppressed contribution, and our argument here is not the racial phenotype of the Olmec but their inclusion in the curriculum. However, some critics would rather attack the racial features of the Olmec, which are clearly non-European, showing "Negroid" features, yet they are lesser known or not even mentioned in educational discourse. In fact, the NCSS has limited or suppressed information on the Olmec in the curriculum that is mandated for all students to learn (NCSS, 2018).

Many pre-Columbus critics claim that African influences erase the accomplishments of Indigenous people. However, *Indigenous* generally refers to early inhabitants. And the preponderance of the evidence suggests the Olmec were the earliest to arrive in the Americas and therefore are one of the Indigenous groups (Van Sertima, 1976/2003; Vaughn, 1998). In this sense, highlighting the Olmec presence is not an erasure, nor does it undermine the contribution of other groups in the Americas. Instead, it centrally places them in the curriculum. There are many ethnic groups in the Americas, including Aztecs, Mayans, Tainos, Arawaks, etc. While there may be some overlaps to consider, the Olmec were among the first to enter the Americas. As Diehl (2004) suggests, it is likely that the region was home to various cultural groups. However, critics are not necessarily challenging that the Olmec were among the earliest people we know of to inhabit the Americas; rather their fixation is on their race.

These critics are not seriously questioning the fact that the Olmec are not included in the curriculum, and they could be helping to make the case for expanding and correcting the curriculum to include this group. Instead, they want to focus on the race—meaning the Olmec cannot be Black, because in their view, Black-skinned people could not have contributed to civilization in the Americas. As a proper chronology of history and social context of the Americas, all students should know about the Olmec, which would also correct the Columbus narrative and the whitewashing of history.

In light of this, this chapter explores the educational implications of the Olmec and their civilization, which the historical record reveals as the oldest in the Americas. We address the omission of the Olmec in education and discuss including them in curriculum development in an attempt to unbleach the curriculum. The preponderance of the evidence suggests that indeed the Olmec was the earliest civilization in the Americas, which is not being challenged. This chapter argues for its inclusion in the curriculum.

In this sense, it is important again to highlight Stirling's (1943) report, as he was one of the earliest people to do archaeological research on the Olmec. His report on the stone monuments of southern Mexico in the Smithsonian Institution's *Bureau of American Ethnology Bulletin* states:

> Despite the scant attention that it has received until recently, the site has been known to archeologists for nearly three-quarters of a century. As early as 1869, J. M. Melgar published an account of several excursions to a place neighboring San Andres Tuxtla in which he referred to certain excavations of a cabeza colosal (Melgar, 1869). Two years later he released a study dealing with the antiquity and origin of the giant head in which he emphasized its "Ethiopian" features, features which have since been identified with the style of art called Olmec (Melgar, 1871). Thereafter, the Cabeza Colosal de Hueyapan (so named from the old Hacienda, though actually much closer to the village of Tres Zapotes than to the modern village of Hueyapan) had won a permanent place in the register of Mexican archeological monuments. (Stirling, 1943, p. 7)

Per Stirling's suggestion, the "Ethiopian," which is a Greek word meaning "burnt of skin" or "Black," features he noted with a broad nose and full lips are generally considered a Black profile. Nevertheless, whether some believe these to be Native or Black features is not the point; the point is that they were here before Columbus (1492), and students, teachers, and citizens should know about this civilization and its contributions. It should be included in the curriculum. Yet, in the 2018 revision of the National Council for the Social Studies' *National Curriculum Standards for Social Studies*, the contributions of the Olmec, the oldest civilization in Mesoamerica (the region from Central Mexico to Central America), are marginalized (NCSS, 2018; Talley-Matthews & Wiggan, 2018; Van Sertima, 1976/2003; Wiggan et al., 2020). There is limited information on them included in the curriculum.

While considerable research addresses the pre-Columbus presence of the Olmec in Mexico (Barton, 2001; Coe et al., 2019; Diehl, 2004; Van Sertima, 1976/2003; Weircinski, 1972), few studies explore these findings relative to their implications for unbleaching and expanding social studies discourse and curriculum development to promote greater inclusion and DEI in U.S. schools (Kamugisha, 2001; J. E. King & Swartz, 2014; Ladson-Billings, 2003; M'Bantu, 2019; Talley-Matthews & Wiggan, 2018; Wiggan et al., 2020; Woodson, 1933/2006). This chapter is important in that it connects the Olmec and their pioneering work in the Americas to curriculum design. It also establishes the Olmec as developers of the first writing system and builders of the first step pyramids in the Americas.

Thus, unbleaching helps to counter master narratives of great European discoverers and whitewashing history. As a conduit of whitening up history, there is the danger of a single story, which generally emphasizes a European ethos (Adichie, 2009). The single story shows people who is important, who is worth knowing, and who has power. To disrupt this oppressive practice, the contributions of the Olmec provide a counternarrative to the single story and master-scripting that places Columbus, who was actually an enslaver

(Clarke, 1995; Columbus, 1847, 2004), as a "discoverer" of the New World, while repositioning the beginning of non-European history in the Americas to the enslavement period. Hence, this book makes a purposeful attempt to contribute to the literature on multicultural curriculum development (Banks, 2010; Clarke, 1995; Grant, 2015; Milner, 2013; Sleeter & Grant, 1999).

This specific chapter helps to unbleach the curriculum and centrally place the contributions of the Olmec civilization. It also explores Olmec presence and influence and the educational implications for teacher practitioners, scholars, and parents in U.S. schools. Unbleaching is an asset-based approach to disrupt the whitewashing of history while centering the unique contributions of oppressed groups. The Columbus discovery narrative whitewashes the history of the Americas, and as such, the Olmec contribution helps to upend this story and unbleach the curriculum.

UNBLEACHING THE OLMEC CIVILIZATION

The early influence of the Olmec civilization is well documented (Barton, 2001; Coe et al., 2019; Diehl, 2004; M'Bantu, 2019; Rashidi, 2016; Van Sertima, 1976/2003; Weircinski, 1972). In *They Came Before Columbus*, Van Sertima (1976/2003) provided evidence that non-Europeans made voyages to and inhabited the New World before Columbus (Columbus, 1847, 2004; Kamugisha, 2001; Van Sertima, 1976/2003; Vaughn, 1998). Van Sertima's findings are similar to the Smithsonian Institution's *Bureau of American Ethnology Bulletin* 138, which noted that the Olmec appear to be "Negroid" and have "Ethiopic" features (Stirling, 1943).

Serving as associate professor of Africana studies at Rutgers University, Dr. Ivan Van Sertima specialized in the African presence in the Americas before Columbus (Rutgers, n.d.). Born in Guyana, South America, Van Sertima studied at the School of Oriental and African Studies at London University (Rutgers, n.d.). His distinguished career included working as a literary critic, a linguist, and an anthropologist. He was the founding editor of the *Journal of African Civilizations*, which aims to transform how African history is viewed and taught. Known for *They Came Before Columbus*, Van Sertima also published *Blacks in Science: Ancient and Modern* (1983), *Black Women in Antiquity* (1984), *The African Presence in Early Asia* (1985), *The African Presence in Early Europe* (1985), *Great Black Leaders, Ancient and Modern* (1988), and *Egypt: Child of Africa* (1994).

As a trained linguist and anthropologist, Van Sertima researched the significant contributions of the Olmec, receiving numerous accolades and international recognition for his work, including the Clarence L. Holte Literary Prize in 1981 for outstanding research (New York Public Library

Archives and Manuscripts, 2020; *New York Times*, 1981). Coe et al. (2019), in *Mexico: From the Olmecs to the Aztecs*, notes that the dates for Olmec civilization vary according to the location, with the site of San Lorenzo in the Early Formative Period (1800–1000 B.C.E.) and the site of La Venta in the Middle Formative Period (1200–400 B.C.E.), and with 800 B.C.E. being the beginning of the most influential period. Based on radioactive carbon dating and archaeological findings, the preponderance of the evidence confirms that Olmec civilization is the oldest in Mesoamerica (Coe et al., 2019; Diehl, 2004; Van Sertima, 1976/2003).

According to Diehl (2004), the Olmec civilization's creation of grand architectural complexes, nucleated towns and cities, and exquisite stonework reflect their sophisticated political, economic, and religious systems. Van Sertima (1976/2003) challenges the master narrative that only European explorers traveled the world, which can help to unbleach the curriculum (Coe et al., 2019; M'Bantu, 2019; Stirling, 1943; Van Sertima, 1976/2003; Vaughn, 1998; Weircinski, 1972).

Early trade routes also support the non-European presence before Columbus (Coe et al., 2019; Kamugisha, 2001; Van Sertima, 1976/2003). Archaeologist Clarence Weiant (Kamugisha, 2001) supports Van Sertima's findings, noting:

> Van Sertima's work is a summary of six or seven years of meticulous research based upon archaeology, Egyptology, African history, oceanography, geology, astronomy, botany, rare Arabic and Chinese manuscripts, the letters and journals of early American explorers and the observations of physical anthropologists. . . . As one who has been immersed in Mexican archaeology for some 40 years and who participated in the excavation of the first of the giant heads, I must confess I am thoroughly convinced of the soundness of van Sertima's conclusions. (Weiant, 1977, p. 2)

In "Ancient Nubian Blacks in the Western World," Vaughn (1998) concurs with Van Sertima's report that people who were phenotypically non-White made technological advancements in the Americas such as the arts of mummification and pyramid building, and the skills needed to transport massive blocks of stone long distances are clearly present in Olmec civilization (Van Sertima, 1976/2003; Vaughn, 1998). According to Vaughn (1998), when Mexicans discovered the first stone heads:

> These colossal heads were over eight feet in height and weighed over 10 tons each. The colossal heads were carbon dated to 800 B.C. and all have typical Nubian features including full lips, fleshy noses, and Africoid facial contours. The ancient Egyptian harbor at Tanis is the only other place in the world with colossal heads of Nubian blacks. (p. A8)

Again, the point here is not the phenotype of the Olmec but their omission from the curriculum. While some researchers contest the validity of the Olmec civilization (Anderson, 2016; Diehl, 2001; Haslip-Viera et al., 1997; Ortiz de Montellano et al., 1997), the historical record reveals that they were in the Americas centuries before Columbus (Clarke, 1977, 1979; Diop, 1974; Melgar y Serrano, 1869a, 1869b, 1869c, 1871; Van Sertima, 1976/2003; Wiggan et al., 2020). Over the last century, the preponderance of the evidence confirms that Columbus was not a discoverer, yet these early pioneers in the Americas are largely omitted in the curriculum.

While some debate the Olmec's phenotypical features, as shown in Figure 5.1, the profile of their lips, nose, and head are clearly non-White and would perhaps be considered Black in America, particularly with the racialized one-drop rule, which stated that anyone with one drop of Black or African blood is considered Black (Hickman, 1996). Haslip-Viera et al. (1997) contest whether people with Black skin could have contributed to civilization in the Americas. Readers can draw their own conclusions based on the archaeological and anthropological evidence. Sifford (2019) contends that the earliest recordings of the non-European presence in Mesoamerica are visually recorded in artifacts crafted by Indigenous artists-scribes, thus displaying their ethnic diversity.

Key findings such as the presence of art forms and evidence of cultural artifacts, as well as organized sport, were found in several archaeological expeditions in San Lorenzo, La Venta, Tres Zapotes, and other parts of Olmec territory (Barton, 2001; Coe et al., 2019; Cooper, 2014; Grove, 2014; Vaughn, 1998). This highlights the importance of unbleaching the Olmec civilization and providing an accurate account of their contributions to the history of the Americas and the world (J. E. King & Swartz, 2014, 2015; Talley-Matthews & Wiggan, 2018; Watson-Vandiver & Wiggan, 2018).

While artifacts including the colossal heads and jadeite sculptures were discovered in Mexico, further evidence of the Olmec presence is found in Honduras, Costa Rica, Guatemala, and El Salvador (Diehl, 2004; Inomata et al., 2013; Joyce & Henderson, 2010). In his field study "Stone Monuments of Southern Mexico," Stirling (1943) reports the following:

> The practice of carving and erecting large stone monuments was one of the conspicuous achievements of the aborigines of tropical America, from northwestern South America to and including a considerable area of southern Mexico. ... Although the art styles employed and the nature of the monuments differ considerably through this rather large region, it seems evident that a certain interrelationship exists, an understanding of which should cast considerable light on the chronologies and pre-Columbian cultural exchanges between the

two continents, especially since the monument-distribution area involves most of the high-culture centers of the New World. (p. 1)

Stirling (1943) supports the vast influence of Olmec civilization in the region. Furthermore, Diehl (2004) reports that pre-Columbian Honduras served as a cultural borderland between various Mesoamerican cultures. Revealing that Olmec art forms were found in Honduras in the 19th century dating back to the Early Formative Period (1800–1000 B.C.E.), Joyce and Henderson (2010) address why "Olmec"-style Honduran objects were present in the country at the time and what this meant to inhabitants. According to Diehl (2004), the Olmec significantly influenced Honduras between 1000 and 600 B.C.E.

THE OLMEC PRESENCE AND UNBLEACHING THE CURRICULUM

The historical record includes anthropological and archaeological artifacts along with considerable research that confirms the influence of Olmec civilization in Mesoamerica (Coe et al., 2019; Diehl, 2004; Grove, 2014; Stirling, 1955; Van Sertima, 1976/2003; Weircinski, 1972). Yet efforts to suppress, withhold, and omit this information from the social studies standards indicate a phenomenon of miseducation that Carter G. Woodson warned against in his seminal work, *The Mis-education of the Negro* (Woodson, 1933/2006). By *miseducation*, Woodson (1933/2006) referred to the indoctrination and the influence of European thinking under the guise of education and its detrimental effects on all learners. An ensuing result is curriculum violence, which Ighodaro and Wiggan (2011) describe as the deliberate manipulation of academic programming in a manner that ignores or compromises the intellectual and psychological well-being of learners.

Failure to teach accurate accounts of human contributions sharply diverges from the premise of unbleaching the history of the Olmec to advance DEI (Ighodaro & Wiggan, 2011; Woodson, 1933/2006). Thus, unbleaching provides a framework for incorporating missing elements in social studies discourse—the contributions of the oldest Mesoamerican civilization. Van Sertima (1976/2003) repositions commonly held ideas regarding the teaching of Black history in America by noting:

[The] African presence in the Olmec world demonstrated that the African first entered the Western Hemisphere not as chattels, not as property, not as merchandise, not as enslaved people, but as masters in control of their own destinies. (p. 365)

As such, unbleaching can expand the conceptualization of early non-European history beyond transatlantic slavery. Therefore, including Olmec contributions in the social studies curriculum and urban education can help expand the curriculum and student learning and outcomes. R. Evans (2017) notes:

> The thought that Africans may have preceded Europeans such as Columbus to what is now America upends all conventional thinking on how, when and in what status Africans first arrived on these shores. The thesis that those who were among the first to discover the Southwest may have been African or of African descent is a revelation that changes, for some, the entire paradigm of prehistoric life in the part of the world that is now Mexico and Texas. (p. 1)

In this sense, all students, not just African Americans, should understand precolonial history and the influence of Olmec civilization (Asante, 1990; Banks, 2010; Gay, 2018; Hilliard, 1998; Sleeter & Grant, 1999). Without this reconceptualization and expansion of curricula, practitioners fail to provide students with a factual account of American history that expands beyond commonly taught narratives regarding slavery and colonialism as the starting point for non-Europeans in the Americas (Adichie, 2009; Akbar, 1998; Wiggan, 2015). This type of miseducation can be psychologically damaging for all students (Akbar, 1998; Ighodaro & Wiggan, 2011; Loewen, 2008; Woodson, 1933/2006).

Even though there is archaeological and historical evidence to support it, the omission of Olmec civilization in the social studies standards leaves a void in the historical record (Coe et al., 2019; Diehl, 2004; Grove, 2014; Van Sertima, 1976/2003; Weircinski, 1972). Furthermore, Kamugisha (2001) reports:

> Ivan van Sertima's thesis represents a mobilization of the ancient past to critique the contemporary "mis-education" of Africana people, and its articulation of Africans as historical agents has tremendous value for popular understandings of the ancient history of the people of the Americas. (p. 237)

The minimization and marginalization of the contributions of Olmec civilization is a pressing concern because these omissions from the National Council for Social Studies curriculum standards represent harmful practices for students and educators alike (Crocco & Costigan, 2007; Ighodaro & Wiggan, 2011; J. E. King & Swartz, 2014, 2015; NCSS, 2018; Woodson, 1933/2006).

The National Curriculum Standards for Social Studies: A Framework for Teaching, Learning, and Assessment addresses the content, pedagogical knowledge, skills, and dispositions needed to prepare social studies teachers (NCSS, 2018). This is not an attack on the NCSS, which has improved. Yet there is a greater need to expand DEI work to address curricular omissions.

Upon close examination, the NCSS standards do not adequately reflect a culturally inclusive perspective on world civilizations, particularly historically marginalized groups like the Olmec. According to NCSS curriculum standards (2018):

> The civic mission of Social Studies demands the inclusion of all students—addressing cultural, linguistic, and learning diversity that includes similarities and differences based on race, ethnicity, language, religion, gender, sexual orientation, exceptional learning needs, and other educationally and personally significant characteristics of learners. Diversity among learners embodies the democratic goal of embracing pluralism to make Social Studies classrooms laboratories of democracy. (p. 9)

The findings on the Olmec help support multicultural practices and DEI to inform the NCSS national standards (Coe et al., 2019; Grove, 2014; Kamugisha, 2001; NCSS, 2018; Van Sertima, 1976/2003; Vaughn, 1998). Without unbleaching and an inclusive account of history that accurately reflects the contributions of all people, particularly those traditionally left on the margins, social studies education contributes to miseducation (Ighodaro & Wiggan, 2011; Rickford, 2016; Woodson, 1933/2006). This chapter emphasizes the need to unbleach the curriculum to include their contributions.

UNBLEACHING THE OLDEST CIVILIZATION IN THE AMERICAS

Unbleaching holds significant implications for urban education and multicultural curriculum development. Data analysis of primary sources reveals that the Olmec civilization is indeed the oldest in the Americas, and artifacts that document this rich history—colossal stone heads, step pyramids, writing systems, and art forms—are on display today in museums in Mexico and around the world (Barton, 2001; Coe et al., 2019; Diehl, 2004; Grove, 2014; M'Bantu, 2019; Rashidi, 2016). While the first Olmec head was discovered by a Mexican farmer in 1862, much of the credit for uncovering their artifacts is attributed to Matthew Stirling, who headed the National Geographic Society–Smithsonian Institution expeditions during the 1930s and 1940s at Tres Zapotes, La Venta, and San Lorenzo (Coe et al., 2019). In its heyday, San Lorenzo had over 10,000 inhabitants and had far-reaching influence in the region. In *Mexico: From the Olmecs to the Aztecs*, Coe et al. (2019) report:

> San Lorenzo had first been settled by 1800 BCE, perhaps by the Mixe-Zoqueans from Soconusco, but by 1500 BCE had become thoroughly Olmec. For the next 500 years San Lorenzo was several times larger than any other settlement in

Mesoamerica; there was in fact nothing quite like it before or during its apogee. . . . San Lorenzo, therefore, was Mesoamerica's first urban civilization, and probably the very first one in all of the Americas. (pp. 66–67)

Among the numerous Early Formative (1800–1000 B.C.E.) sculptures found in San Lorenzo, ten colossal heads "are up to 9 ft 4 in. (2.85 m) in height and weigh up to 25 tons; it seems likely that they are all portraits of mighty Olmec rulers, with flat-faced, thick lipped features" (Coe et al., 2019, p. 69).

Colossal head number four, found at San Lorenzo, is on display at the Smithsonian National Museum of Natural History in Washington, DC (Smithsonian National Museum of Natural History, n.d.) (see Figure 5.2). Multiple colossal heads are displayed at museums and sites throughout Mexico and the world (Stirling, 1955). Discovered by Stirling in 1946, this statue is known as El Rey, or "The King," because of his majestic appearance (Stirling, 1955). Traits such as the broad noses and thick lips are common among the Olmec busts. Each of the 17 Olmec heads that have been discovered has distinctive similarities that connect them to a non-White or Black ethos (M'Bantu, 2019; Melgar y Serrano, 1869a, 1869c; Rashidi, 2016; Stirling, 1955). In the context of unbleaching the curriculum, this emphasizes cultural continuity with Ethiopia, the birthplace of humanity. These historical contributions can enhance classroom instruction for all learners.

Figure 5.2. Olmec Colossal Head #4, San Lorenzo. (Source: Wikicommons)

Figure 5.3. Replica of Olmec Colossal Head Donated by Mexico to Ethiopia. (Source: Authors)

As such, in 2010, Mexico donated a replica of an Olmec colossal head to Ethiopia (see Figure 5.3), which is on display at the National Museum of Ethiopia (National Museum of Ethiopia at Addis Ababa, 2019). In effect, this represents Mexico's acknowledgment of the presumed influence of Africa on Olmec civilization (National Museum of Anthropology of Mexico City, 2019).

After San Lorenzo's fall, during the Middle Formative Period (1200–400 B.C.E.), La Venta, Tabasco, was an active Olmec site where Stirling and others discovered a clay pyramid that was 110 feet tall (Coe et al., 2019; Stirling, 1943, 1955). Dating circa 400 B.C.E., the Great Olmec Pyramid at La Venta, one of the earliest known in Mesoamerica, is one of the tallest monuments of this era. Gonzalez Lauk (1988) theorizes that originally this was a rectangular step pyramid; however, its shape today is largely a result of 2,500 years of erosion and overgrowth of forestry. Similarly, Diehl (2004) indicates that a mound pyramid bearing similarities to other Olmec structures is present in El Salvador.

BLEACHING, WHITEWASHING, AND DEI SOCIAL JUSTICE EFFORTS

Curriculum development has the potential to bring about equity and excellence in education. Thus, this chapter explores the educational implications of unbleaching the social studies curriculum to include the Olmec. Findings indicate that Olmec civilization is the oldest in the Americas; archaeological and anthropological evidence indicates that the Olmec predated Columbus's arrival to the Americas as early as 800 B.C.E. (Coe et al., 2019; Diehl, 2004; Grove, 2014; Stirling, 1955; Van Sertima, 1976/2003; Weircinski, 1972).

To broaden the contours and content related to teaching about the development of Olmec civilization from an unbleaching framework, this chapter advocates for the inclusion of Olmec contributions in the social studies standards. According to the historical record (albeit suppressed) from as early as the 1800s—made popular by Matthew Stirling and the National Geographic–Smithsonian expeditions between 1939 and 1946—the archaeological evidence presented herein supports the Black or African, or "Ethiopic" (meaning "burnt of skin" or "Black"), as he noted, presence in the Olmec civilization (Coe et al., 2019; Van Sertima, 1976/2003).

Unbleaching places students' cultural backgrounds at the center of their learning, thereby nurturing social consciousness and critical thinking. Making the connection between the Olmec and the influence of African civilizations in their development is intuitive. Furthermore, unbleaching presents an asset-based approach to teaching and learning that can be applied to social studies content to expand DEI and promote greater student academic achievement (Gay, 2018; J. E. King & Swartz, 2018; Ladson-Billings & Tate, 1995). Unbleaching the curriculum helps to reaffirm the history of non-European civilizations like the Olmec (Asante, 1990; Clark, 1977; J. E. King & Swartz, 2014; Talley-Matthews & Wiggan, 2018). The connection between the Olmec and early civilization in the Americas is an area that can be further supported through a corrected curriculum.

For its efficacy and its potential for inclusion, this vital information—the role of the Olmec in American civilization and its connection to Africa—should be included in the revised social studies standards (J. E. King & Swartz, 2014, 2015; NCSS, 2018). Olmec civilization is the oldest in Mesoamerica, and given that considerable archaeological evidence supports this, unbleaching the curriculum and expanding curricular offerings is essential (Coe et al., 2019; Diehl, 2004; J. E. King & Swartz, 2014, 2015; NCSS, 2018).

In this chapter, important archaeological and anthropological evidence confirmed the significance of the Olmec in Mesoamerican history prior to Columbus's arrival. The Olmec presence is confirmed by the presence of 17 colossal heads which are on display at museums in Mexico, the U.S., and around the world (Stirling, 1955). Additional evidence of the Olmec presence includes the development of the earliest form of writing found in the Americas, as well as a calendar system that predates Mayan and Aztec civilizations (Coe et al., 2019; Diehl, 2001, 2004; Van Sertima, 1976/2003). Taken together, these findings provide a rich basis for the development of curriculum and lesson planning that center the contributions of the Olmec within social studies discourse and urban education. Through unbleaching the contribution of the Olmec and incorporating primary source data in curricular content, learners will have a more accurate account of human history, and teachers can create more relevant lesson plans.

Ultimately, this chapter presents implications for teachers, scholars, and parents in U.S. schools who are concerned about quality education that addresses the contributions of all people (Talley-Matthews & Wiggan, 2018; Watson-Vandiver & Wiggan, 2018). To correct miseducation in public schools, it provides perspectives on Olmec civilization as a tool for social studies curriculum development. A clearer understanding of the Olmec contribution to American history expands social studies discourse to improve teacher preparation to promote culturally responsive pedagogical practices (Gay, 2018). Additional studies are needed to address the inclusion of Olmec contributions in the social studies standards published by the NCSS. While this chapter has primarily investigated the marginalization of Olmec civilization in education, more research is needed to address other missing narratives and diverse groups' histories whose omission contributes to miseducation.

CHAPTER SUMMARY

This chapter focused on the contributions of the early Americas, specifically the Olmec civilization. While information about this civilization is neglected or suppressed in education, the chapter presented insights and perspectives that inform teacher pedagogical practices and curricular design. It provided information that helps to unbleach the curriculum to improve student outcomes and enhance DEI in education processes and practices. The next chapter addresses the Black presence in Europe and Asia and its curricular and pedagogical implications.

Chapter 6

Black and African Contributions in Asia and Europe

History is a light that illuminates the past, and a key that unlocks the door to the future.

—*Runoko Rashidi*

In the previous chapters, we addressed the marginalization of Black contributions in Egypt and the Americas. While expanding this theme, this chapter presents evidence of Black or African contributions in Asia and Europe. Using a global perspective, the chapter explores how these omissions can enhance an unbleached curriculum and DEI processes and practices in education.

For students in U.S. public schools, a bleached and whitewashed curriculum omits or suppresses key contributions, which generally results in curriculum violence and miseducation. In this chapter, using primary sources from historians such as Herodotus and Diodorus, we expand our treatise on the implications of omitted contributions by exploring an African or Black presence in Asia and Europe. Evidence of Africans in literary works in ancient Europe such as Hannibal, Othello, and Alessandro de' Medici is important and worth noting. However, students in U.S. public schools are often taught this literature without exploring their true social and historical context. For instance, William Shakespeare's *The Tragedy of Othello: The Moor of Venice* is a play about a Moor (a Black) military commander and general of the Venetian army who defended Cyprus against invasion by Ottoman Turks (Braxton, 1990; K. W. Evans, 1969; Shakespeare, 1883).

Some literary scholars contest that Othello's Moorish (African) heritage is central to his character (Braxton, 1990; E. D. Jones, 1965). Without the proper contextualization of multicultural contributions in literature, there can be misalignment with facts. In the context of literature and social studies, for example, omitting Othello's ethnicity and/or race from curricula distorts the social context regarding Shakespeare's writings (Braxton, 1990). In fact, K. W. Evans (1969) notes that "no analysis of the play can be adequate if it ignores the factor of race" (p. 125). The Moors and their African origins are discussed in greater detail in a later section of this chapter. Information regarding the Moors and their part in world history is often silenced or marginalized in the social studies curriculum.

While the National Council for the Social Studies publishes social studies standards, a revision that reflects the African contributions in Europe and Asia can expand multiculturalism. Notwithstanding, omitting this information prevents students from having deep exposure to primary sources. This is an area that the National Council for the Social Studies, the Common Core State Standards (CCSS), and others claim to value (NCSS, 2017, 2018). However, the accurate representation of Black or African contributions to humanity is still insufficient in most curricular standards. While this book does not seek to attack these national frameworks, we do hope to expand the scope to address historical accuracy and whitewashing with proper contextualization and unbleaching of curricula.

This chapter discusses these and other omissions of African or Black contributions to world history. While the NCSS revised its social studies curriculum standards in 2017, an improvement, they still do not fully reflect the contributions of marginalized groups to world history (NCSS, 2018). Consequently, a major cause of miseducation is the single story, an incomplete narrative that largely omits multicultural perspectives, which is often a staple of public school curriculum development. This practice undermines students' growth and development, as well as their achievement. As discussed in chapter 1, there are generally low levels of student achievement in reading and mathematics across all school types. Thus, a corrected and unbleached curriculum that includes the contributions of all learners has the highest potential of improving student outcomes (Banks, 2010; Gay, 2018; Ladson-Billings, 2016). Even so, all students would benefit from having a corrected curriculum. Providing a more accurate and comprehensive view of history and the contributions of Blacks and Africans can address DEI issues and promote social justice in public education. Moreover, connecting these omissions to the NCSS social studies standards and themes can improve the curriculum for all learners. As such, we begin by exploring perspectives on the Black or African presence in Europe and Asia from ancient Greek historians.

UNBLEACHING AND THE AFRICAN CONTRIBUTION TO WORLD HISTORY

Anyone who writes on or studies ancient history or antiquities should familiarize themselves with the works of Herodotus, regarded by most as the father of European history, and Diodorus Siculus (Diodorus), a towering ancient European historian (Asheri et al., 2007; Lateiner, 2016). Both Herodotus and Diodorus reference the works of Ephorus, author of *Historai* or *The History*. However, Ephorus's writings have not survived.

Notwithstanding, Herodotus wrote *The Histories* (Rawlinson & Wilkinson, 1861), which is considered the first European narrative history book. Herodotus's *Histories* is the first historical literature in Europe, but not the rest of the world. As discussed in chapter 3, *The Teachings of PtahHotep* (2300 B.C.E.) is the oldest book in the world and predates *The Histories* by 1800 years. Yet this book is rarely mentioned in social studies standards in U.S. public schools. In fact, Egyptian texts such as *The Book of the Coming Forth by Day*, also called *The Book of the Dead*, dated circa 2000 B.C.E., is the oldest religious book in the world (Budge, 1855).

Additionally, *The Law of Hammurabi*, 1792 B.C.E., a text that set out moral codes and laws intended to govern Babylonian society, is much older than Herodotus's work (Harper, 1999; Vincent, 1904). Nevertheless, Herodotus's *Histories* are important and worth discussing, as he presented firsthand accounts of his travels as he wrote. Herodotus traveled to the Persian Empire, to Egypt, Libya, Syria, Babylonia, Susa in Elam (modern-day Iran), Lydia, and Phrygia (modern-day Turkey). Additionally, he journeyed up the Hellespont (now Dardanelles) to Byzantium, to Thrace (Southeast Europe) and Macedonia (Balkan Peninsula), and traveled northward to beyond the Danube and to Scythia eastward along the northern shores of the Black Sea as far as the Don River (Rawlinson & Wilkinson, 1861). When describing ancient Egyptians, Herodotus notes:

> Before I heard any mention of the fact from others, I had remarked it myself. After the thought had struck me, I made inquiries on the subject both in Colchis and in Egypt, and I found that the Colchians had a more distinct recollection of the Egyptians, than the Egyptians had of them. Still the Egyptians said that they believed the Colchians to be descended from the army of Sesostris. My own conjectures were founded, first, on the fact that they are black-skinned and have woolly hair, which certainly amounts to but little, since several other nations are so too; but further and more especially, on the circumstance that the Colchians, the Egyptians, and the Ethiopians, are the only nations who have practised circumcision from the earliest times. The Phoenicians and the Syrians of Palestine themselves confess that they learnt the custom of the Egyptians;

and the Syrians who dwell about the rivers Thermodon and Parthenius, as well as their neighbours the Macronians, say that they have recently adopted it from the Colchians. Now these are the only nations who use circumcision, and it is plain that they all imitate herein the Egyptians. With respect to the Ethiopians, indeed, I cannot decide whether they learnt the practice of the Egyptians, or the Egyptians of them—it is undoubtedly of very ancient date in Ethiopia—but that the others derived their knowledge of it from Egypt is clear to me from the fact that the Phoenicians, when they come to have commerce with the Greeks, cease to follow the Egyptians in this custom, and allow their children to remain uncircumcised. (Rawlinson & Wilkinson, 1861, p. 138)

Herodotus's observations are important as he documents the Egyptians as Black and notes that there was a Black presence in Europe. Herodotus references Sesostris (see Figure 6.1), who was also known as Senusret I and Senwosret I (Egyptian Museum, n.d.). After co-ruling with his father Amenemhet I, Senusret (Sesostris) ruled as the second pharaoh of the 12th Dynasty of Egypt. His conquest of Nubia and his expeditions against Libya are noteworthy historical feats of his reign. Herodotus also details the expanse of ancient Egypt. Sesostris I named the land south of the second cataract Kush (also spelled Cush) (Rawlinson & Wilkinson, 1861). Herodotus's accounts of the Black presence in Europe and Africa are important, as he is largely considered "the Father of History" in Europe.

In fact, it is well documented that ancient Egyptians were maritime people, with "foreign trade with Africa, Asia, and the Mediterranean" (Mokhtar, 1981, p. 140). Herodotus reports that African merchants were developing trade in the Red Sea and Indian Ocean in antiquity (Chang'ach, 2014). This is supported through primary source writings. When describing the Moroccan coast, Herodotus notes in *The Histories*, volume 4:

> The Carthaginians also inform us about a part of Africa and its inhabitants beyond the straits of Gibraltar. When they reach this country, they unload their goods and arrange them on the beach; they then return to their ships and send up a smoke signal. When the natives see the smoke, they come down to the sea and place a quantity of gold in exchange for the goods and then retire. The Carthaginians then come ashore again and examine the gold that has been left; if they think it represents the value of the goods they collect it and sail away; if not, they return to their ships and wait until the natives have added sufficient gold to satisfy them. (440 B.C.E./2014, paras. 1–3)

Like Herodotus, Diodorus, a highly respected Greek historian, provides documentation on the early Black presence.

Diodorus lived during the reign of Caesar Augustus (27 B.C.E.–14 C.E.), when the Romans succeeded the Greeks as a superpower and colonized North

Figure 6.1. King Sesostris I. (Source: Wikimedia Commons)

Africa and some of western Asia (Diodorus, 60/59 B.C.E./1790, Book I). As a type of statesman, this means that Diodorus would have been able to travel throughout the Roman Empire, and he would have access to libraries that were taken under Roman rule. He also spent several years in Egypt, which was considered the prized colony of the Romans. Diodorus's early work, in addition to writing about European history, includes discussions on Egypt, India, and Abdera (near the Hellespont, a strait in Turkey) in the context of world history and civilizations.

Diodorus writes on the early history and mythology of Egypt, Asia, India, Arabia, Ethiopia, and Libya. He also writes about the Greeks. As a historian, Diodorus is best known for his 40-volume work *Bibliotheca Historica* (Diodorus, 60/59 B.C.E./1868), which explored the history of the Mediterranean region in ancient times, 60/59 B.C.E. The 15 remaining volumes of *Bibliotheca Historica* give a fairly comprehensive view of world history that includes the African presence in Egypt and Ethiopia. In Diodorus's Book I, he writes almost exclusively on Egypt, as he was intrigued by this great civilization. Diodorus's assessment of Egypt is worth documenting here. When addressing Homer, author of *The Iliad* and *The Odyssey* (700–750 B.C.E.), the first recorded book in Europe, as being influenced by the Egyptians, Diodorus notes:

> And as proof of the presence of Homer in Egypt they adduce various pieces of evidence, and especially the healing drink which brings forgetfulness of all past evils, which was given by Helen to Telemachus in the home of Menelaus. For it is manifest that the poet had acquired exact knowledge of the "nepenthic" drug which he says Helen brought from Egyptian Thebes, given her by Polydamna the wife of Thon; for, they allege, even to this day the women of this city use this powerful remedy, and in ancient times, they say, a drug to cure anger and sorrow was discovered exclusively among the women of Diospolis; but Thebes and Diospolis, they add, are the same city. . . . Likewise, the myths which are related about the dalliance of Zeus and Hera and of their journey to Ethiopia he also got from Egypt; for each year among the Egyptians the shrine of Zeus is carried across the river into Libya and then brought back some days later, as if the god were arriving from Ethiopia; and as for the dalliance of these deities, in their festal gatherings the priests carry the shrines of both to an elevation that has been strewn with flowers of every description. (60/59 B.C.E./1790, Book I, pp. 333–335)

Diodorus explains that Homer takes aspects of Egyptian mythology and uses them directly in his work *The Odyssey*. As Diodorus notes, the same themes and characters in the Egyptian story appear in *The Odyssey* with different names (Diodorus, 60/59 B.C.E./1790, Book I, pp. 333–335). While *The Odyssey* is regularly taught as part of the curriculum in U.S. K–12 public schools and in higher education, there is no reference to African influences or, more importantly, African literature in the curriculum. This is symptomatic of the bleaching that occurs in the U.S. public school curriculum, which speaks to the importance of unbleaching the curriculum.

As previously noted, the U.S. public school curriculum does not center multicultural perspectives (Banks, 1993a, 1993b; Banks & Banks, 2010; Byford & Russell, 2007; Grant, 2015). In this way, exploring the contributions of Africans across the globe can provide insight for DEI processes and practices. Thus, unbleaching—the process of disrupting Eurocentrism and systems of oppression that undermine, suppress, falsify, dehumanize, and marginalize non-Europeans and their perspectives and contributions as conduits for creating and maintaining power and privilege—is necessary. Furthermore, expanding the curriculum to include a more inclusive view of world history is a necessary mandate for appropriate expansion of the NCSS Revised Social Studies Standards. This should not be viewed as an attack but as a necessary suggestion to expand and be more inclusive. While used as a framework for teachers, schools, districts, states, and other nations as a tool for curriculum alignment and development, the NCSS standards can be expanded to include more multicultural perspectives.

There are 10 themes in social studies: (1) culture; (2) time, continuity, and change; (3) people, places, and environment; (4) individual development and identity; (5) individuals, groups, and institutions; (6) power, authority, and governance; (7) production, distribution, and consumption; (8) science, technology, and society; (9) global connections; and (10) civic ideals and practices. These themes and the accompanying standards are relevant to the study of the African contribution in Europe and Asia within courses such as geography, world history, political science, civics, and economics. The official definition of social studies, according to the NCSS, is:

> The integrated study of the social sciences and humanities to promote civic competence. Within the school program, social studies provides coordinated, systematic study drawing upon such disciplines as anthropology, archaeology, economics, geography, history, law, philosophy, political science, psychology, religion, and sociology, as well as appropriate content from the humanities, mathematics, and natural sciences. The primary purpose of social studies is to help young people make informed and reasoned decisions for the public good as citizens of a culturally diverse, democratic society in an interdependent world. (2018, p. 3)

In this way, the information contained in this chapter can help inform social studies curriculum development for teachers, educators, parents, and the community.

More specifically, the NCSS themes of (1) culture; (2) time, continuity, and change; (3) people, places, and environments; (6) power, authority, and governance; and (9) global connections directly correspond to the main tenets of this chapter. Theme (1) culture (NCSS) emphasizes the need for understanding

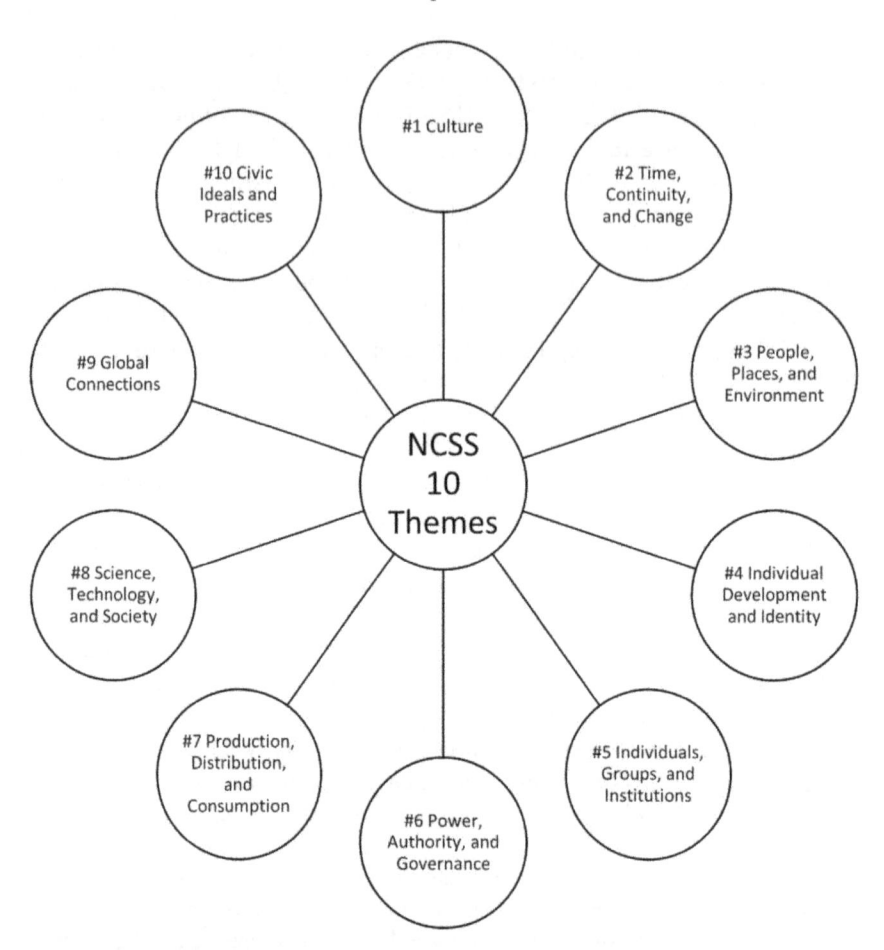

Figure 6.2. NCSS 10 Themes. (Source: NCSS, 2018)

what culture is and what role it plays in human and societal development. Theme (2) time, continuity, and change (NCSS) addresses studying the past to learn about the roots of our social, political, and economic systems. This study of the past and its legacy can also help inform how perspectives about the past differ, and to what extent these differences inform contemporary ideas and actions. An examination of Herodotus's *Histories* and Diodorus Siculus's *Bibliotheca Historica* provides a background for understanding the importance of the past in contextualizing contemporary events. The learner's place in human history is further established through a clearer exploration of the past that does not marginalize multicultural perspectives.

Both Herodotus and Diodorus present a view of history that is fairly comprehensive in its exploration of the timeline of historical events within the period, and they capture the African influences therein (Diodorus, 60/59

B.C.E./1790, Book I). Theme (3) people, places, and environments (NCSS) is useful in understanding the African Diaspora and how maps, globes, geographic tools, and geospatial technologies contribute to the understanding of people, places, and environments from a historical and contemporary lens. To make the connection to the curriculum and the need for reform, excerpts from *The Histories* and *Bibliotheca Historica* help the reader trace the movement of African people and their subsequent influence on world civilization. Theme (6) power, authority, and governance (NCSS) is the study of how people create, interact with, and change structures of power, authority, and governance.

As shown in the primary source documents below, the African influences in Europe and Asia have been documented in some of the earliest historical records. Theme (9) global connections (NCSS), explores the impact of past global connections and how ideas spread between societies in an interconnected world. For students in U.S. public schools, a curriculum that clearly makes the connection between the origins of human history and how the movements of Black and African people are still present can potentially improve student performance. Also important here is the influence of increasing global interdependence on patterns of international migration. In the exploration of the evolution of human history and the African presence in Europe and Asia, the themes noted above are particularly relevant to NCSS standards and unbleaching the curriculum. In the next section, we address in greater detail how an understanding of the origins of human history can contribute to unbleaching the curriculum.

UNBLEACHING AND THE DEVELOPMENT OF HUMAN HISTORY

Buttressing the Greek thinkers Herodotus's and Diodorus's observations of Black and African contributions and presence in Europe and Asia, science has shown that all humans share 99.9% of the same mitochondrial DNA (NSF, 2001; Shared DNA, 2005). These findings affirm that indeed all humans are part of the family tree that started in Africa (National Human Genome Research Institute, 2006/2011; NSF, 2001; Shared DNA, 2005). The historical significance of Africa is important to mention here given the 1974 archaeological discovery of the first human, Lucy (also called Dinkinesh, meaning "you are marvelous" in Amharic), in what is now Ethiopia (Relethford, 2008).

Dating over 4.2 million years, the first human remains indicate the importance of Africa as a critical reference point for the origins of human history. Ethiopia is the cradle of humanity, where the first humans—Dinkinesh and

Ardi—were discovered (Relethford, 2008; Shared DNA, 2005; Wiggan, 2015). Starting at the beginning of the human timeline is intuitive for all learners in that it establishes a human-centric worldview and highlights notable examples of hegemony in education. As noted in *Born in Africa*, more than 20 species of extinct humans have been found in Africa, and groups of Africans possessing skills in early technology, language, and art journeyed to populate the rest of the world (Meredith, 2011). Fossil remains of *Australopithecus afarensis*, known as "Lucy," were first discovered in Ethiopia and Tanzania in the 1970s.

Since the oldest human remains were found in Africa, it is important to note how this influences the flow of world historical development (National Human Genome Research Institute, 2006/2011; NSF, 2001; Shared DNA, 2005; Relethford, 2008; Wiggan, 2015). Thus, the African Diaspora involves the movement of African-descended people around the world. This is especially important regarding the African presence in Asia.

In the article "Great Achievements in Science and Technology in Ancient Africa," published by the American Society for Biochemistry and Molecular Biology, Blatch (2013) notes that precolonial Africans sailed to Asia hundreds of years before Europeans. Similarly, in what is considered a turning-point work, in the 1998 *Proceedings of the National Academy of Sciences*, a consortium of seven major Chinese research groups notes that over 20% of modern China has genetic origins from Africa (Hotz, 1998). This research was sponsored by the Chinese Human Genome Diversity Project, the Human Genetic Center at the University of Texas Health Science Center at Houston, and the National Science Foundation of China (Cavalli-Sforza, 1998). These findings conclude that some of the gene pool in East Asia derives from Africa. However, with the recent advancement of genetic technology, in the newer studies, scientists now suggest that over 97.4% of Chinese genetic makeup derives from early humans who came from Africa, with the rest of the genetic makeup from Neanderthals and Denisovans (discovered in Siberia) (Qiu, 2016). Whether readers accept the earlier research (Hotz, 1998) or the later research on this topic (Qiu, 2016), in any case, the evidence is clear that there is a scientific basis for the African presence in China and generally in Asia.

In relation to human origins, Hotz (1998) notes that humans migrated out of Africa in waves over a million years ago. From there, humans from Africa colonized Europe, the Middle East, and Asia. This is a historical fact on which "everyone agrees" (para. 14). The second wave of migration is often debated. Some historians believe humankind's evolution into sophisticated toolmakers led Africans to regenerate and repopulate (C. R. Johnson, 2009). Others argue that there was no second wave from Africa, and instead the previous generation of Africans evolved into advanced contributors to civilization (Nei & Livshits, 1989; Tishkoff et al., 2009). Notwithstanding, the relationship between Africa and Asia, and Africa's influence on humanity, is supported by research (Nei & Livshits, 1989; Tishkoff et al., 2009). Both the earlier research and the more recent research suggest African roots in China (C. R. Johnson, 2009; Qiu, 2016). This is important historical contextualization to note.

As Michael Gomez (2019) notes in *Reversing Sail: A History of the African Diaspora*, the African Diaspora did not begin with the slave trade but began millennia ago with the dispersal of African culture and the movement of African people. As early as 3500 B.C.E., the ancient Egyptians traded goods with the Sumerians, and:

> by 1700 B.C.E. [were] connected with urban-based civilizations in the Indus valley, the Iranian plateau, and China. Situated in Africa, Egypt was also a global crossroad for various populations and cultures, its participation in this intercontinental zone a major feature of the African Diaspora's opening chapter. (Gomez, 2019, p. 11)

Given this movement, Africans were influential in the historical development of the world. This is not a suggestion to remove any group's contribution from the curriculum, but rather a case for how the omissions can be addressed in a corrected curriculum that is unbleached. In southern Europe and the Near East, many Africans in the ancient world were considered leaders holding prestige and power (Diop, 1974; Gomez, 2019).

Gomez (2019) is not alone in this assertion regarding the historical significance of Africa in the ancient world. As noted, the ancient Greeks also made the same observations. Greek historian Diodorus documents the African presence in Europe (Rawlinson & Wilkinson, 1861). He states that during the reign of Sesostris I (12th Dynasty, 1908–1875 B.C.E.), he and his army entered Arabia, Europe, and much of Asia. Diodorus notes:

> First of all Sesoosis [Sesostris], his companions also accompanying him, was sent by his father with an army into Arabia, where he was subjected to the laborious training of hunting wild animals and, after hardening himself to the privations of thirst and hunger, conquered the entire nation of the Arabs, which had never been enslaved before his day; and then, on being sent to the regions to the west, he subdued the larger part of Libya, though in years still no more than a youth. And when he ascended the throne upon the death of his father, being filled with confidence by reason of his earlier exploits he undertook to conquer the inhabited earth. (60/59 B.C.E./1790, Book I, p. 187)

Diodorus continues:

In the same way he brought all the rest of Asia into subjection as well as most of the Cyclades islands. And after he had crossed into Europe and was on his way through the whole length of Thrace he nearly lost his army through lack of food and the difficult nature of the land. Consequently he fixed the limits of his expedition in Thrace, and set up stelae in many parts of the regions which he had acquired; and these carried the following inscription in the Egyptian writing which is called "sacred": "This land the King of Kings and Lord of Lords, Sesoosis, subdued with his own arms." (60/59 B.C.E./1790, Book I, p. 193)

Further, Diodorus notes:

He dealt gently with all conquered peoples and, after concluding his campaign in nine years, commanded the nations to bring presents each year to Egypt according to their ability, while he himself, assembling a multitude of captives which has never been surpassed and a mass of other booty, returned to his country, having accomplished the greatest deeds of any king of Egypt to his day. (60/59 B.C.E./1790, Book I, p. 195)

Like Diodorus, Herodotus explains that Sesostris I was a king in ancient Egypt who led a military expedition into parts of Europe (see Figure 6.1 above). Regarding the African presence in Asia, Herodotus writes of Pharaoh Sesostris I, king of Egypt. He notes that his army conquered territories in Asia. Herodotus explains:

Passing over these monarchs, therefore, I shall speak of the king who reigned next, whose name was Sesostris. He, the priests said, first of all proceeded in a fleet of ships of war from the Arabian gulf along the shores of the Erythraean sea, subduing the nations as he went, until he finally reached a sea which could not be navigated by reason of the shoals. Hence he returned to Egypt, where, they told me, he collected a vast armament, and made a progress by land across the continent, conquering every people which fell in his way. In the countries where the natives withstood his attack, and fought gallantly for their liberties, he erected pillars, on which he inscribed his own name and country, and how that he had here reduced the inhabitants to subjection by the might of his arms: where, on the contrary, they submitted readily and without a struggle. . . . In this way he traversed the whole continent of Asia, whence he passed on into Europe, and made himself master of Scythia and of Thrace, beyond which countries I do not think that his army extended its march. For thus far the pillars which he erected are still visible, but in the remoter regions they are no longer found. (Rawlinson & Wilkinson, 1861, pp. 136–137)

Herodotus further notes:

Sesostris was king not only of Egypt, but also of Ethiopia. He was the only Egyptian monarch who ever ruled over the latter country. He left, as memorials of his reign, the stone statues which stand in front of the temple of Vulcan, two of which, representing himself and his wife, are thirty cubits in height, while the remaining four, which represent his sons, are twenty cubits. These are the statues, in front of which the priest of Vulcan, very many years afterwards, would not allow Darius the Persian to place a statue of himself; "because," he said, "Darius had not equalled the achievements of Sesostris the Egyptian: for while Sesostris had subdued to the full as many nations as ever Darius had brought under, he had likewise conquered the Scythians, whom Darius had failed to master. It was not fair, therefore, that he should erect his statue in front of the offerings of a king, whose deeds he had been unable to surpass." Darius, they say, pardoned the freedom of this speech. (Rawlinson & Wilkinson, 1861, pp. 137–140)

As Herodotus and Diodorus explain, Sesostris I and other Egyptians had made a presence in Europe and Asia.

As further proof of the African influence, in Book III, Diodorus discusses Ethiopia, African Amazons, Atlantis, and their people. He also discusses the genesis of ideas surrounding God in the context of Africa, and perhaps as an African contribution in early human history. Diodorus explains:

Now the Ethiopians, as historians relate, were the first of all men and the proofs of this statement, they say, are manifest. For that they did not come into their land as immigrants from abroad but were natives of it and so justly bear the name of "autochthones" is, they maintain, conceded by practically all men; furthermore, that those who dwell beneath the noon-day sun were, in all likelihood, the first to be generated by the earth, is clear to all; since, inasmuch as it was the warmth of the sun which, at the generation of the universe. (60/59 B.C.E./1790, Book III, pp. 91–93)

Diodorus further notes:

And they say that they were the first to be taught to honour the gods and to hold sacrifices and processions and festivals and the other rites by which men honour the deity; and that in consequence their piety has been published abroad among all men, and it is generally held that the sacrifices practised among the Ethiopians are those which are the most pleasing to heaven. As witness to this they call upon the poet who is perhaps the oldest and certainly the most venerated among the Greeks; for in the Iliad he represents both Zeus and the rest of the gods with him as absent on a visit to Ethiopia to share in the sacrifices and the banquet which were given annually by the Ethiopians for all the gods together:

> For Zeus had yesterday to Ocean's bounds
> Set forth to feast with Ethiop's faultless men,
> And he was followed there by all the gods.

And they state that, by reason of their piety towards the deity, they manifestly enjoy the favour of the gods, inasmuch as they have never experienced the rule of an invader from abroad; for from all time they have enjoyed a state of freedom and of peace one with another, and although many and powerful rulers have made war upon them, not one of these has succeeded in his undertaking. (60/59 B.C.E./1790, Book III, pp. 91–93)

Diodorus confidently asserts that the Ethiopians, "those who dwell beneath the noon-day sun were, in all likelihood, the first to be generated by the earth"—that is, they were likely the first humans (Diodorus, 60/59 B.C.E./1790, Book III). This directly connects to social studies themes 1, 2, 3, 6, and 9. Diodorus further explains that the region nearest the sun might be the first to bring forth living creatures. This connects with the earlier information presented in this chapter about the 1974 discovery of Lucy (also called Dinkinesh), the oldest human remains found in Ethiopia (NSF, 2001; Relethford, 2008). Regarding the movement of the Ethiopians, Diodorus further notes in Book III:

But there are also a great many other tribes of the Ethiopians, some of them dwelling in the land lying on both banks of the Nile and on the islands in the river, others inhabiting the neighbouring country of Arabia, and still others residing in the interior of Libya. The majority of them, and especially those who dwell along the river, are black in colour and have flat noses and woolly hair. As for their spirit they are entirely savage and display the nature of a wild beast, not so much, however, in their temper as in their ways of living; for they are squalid all over their bodies, they keep their nails very long like the wild beasts, and are as far removed as possible from human kindness to one another; and speaking as they do with a shrill voice and cultivating none of the practices of civilized life as these are found among the rest of mankind, they present a striking contrast when considered in the light of our own customs. (60/59 B.C.E./1790, Book III, p. 105)

Diodorus's (60/59 B.C.E./1868) observations affirm the African connections to the development of world history, bringing attention to its importance in the genesis of humankind and their influence on other nations. An unbleached curriculum including the African contributions to world history underscores the importance of NCSS social studies themes of (1) culture; (2) time, continuity, and change; (3) people, places, and environments; (6) power, authority, and governance; and (9) global connections. Next, we further examine the African presence in Asia by tracing the timeline explained in Diodorus's *Bibliotheca Historica* and noting the artifacts that provide reference for expanding the curriculum and making connections from the past to the present.

UNBLEACHING AND THE AFRICAN PRESENCE IN ASIA

Documentation of the African presence in Asia can expand the curriculum and mitigate bleaching and whitewashing. As such, various artifacts affirm the African presence in Asia and the notable contributions made to civilization. Mokhtar (1981) notes that the search for stone, fibers, and pigments "contributed to the spread of Egyptian techniques to Asia and Africa" (p. 161). In *A History of Ethiopia*, Budge (1928/2015) notes that Herodotus supports the connections between Asians and Ethiopians as he explains that there were people in both places with Black skin and woolly hair. Additionally, Budge finds culture, traditions, and religious practices that link some Asians back to Africa. J. G. Jackson (1939/2017) and Rawlinson (2018) also note that Ethiopians once occupied both Asia and Africa. Sculptures and historical archives describe the Kushite occupation, and eventual colonization, of Mesopotamia around 2800 B.C.E. (Adamo, 2001). In addition to sculptures and art, Mokhtar (1981) notes that many well-known historical artifacts, such as Imhotep's Manuscript (also known as the Edwin Smith Papyrus), highlight the widespread impact of the Egyptians. Chang'ach (2015) explains:

> The Smith Papyrus bears testimony to the skill of the surgeons of ancient Egypt, skill which it would be fair to assume was handed on gradually, in Africa as well as Asia and to classical antiquity, by the doctors who were always attached to Egyptian expeditions to foreign lands. Moreover, it is known that foreign sovereigns, like the Asian prince of Bakhtan, Bactria, or Cambyses himself, brought in Egyptian doctors. (p. 6)

In addition to Imhotep's Manuscript, which is discussed in chapter 4, Henry Creswicke Rawlinson and George Rawlinson also identified African roots in West Asian texts. In their commentary on the *History of Herodotus*, Rawlinson and Rawlinson (1858) contend:

> Recent linguistic discovery tends to show that a Cushite or Ethiopian race did in the earliest times extend itself along the shores of the Southern Ocean from Abyssinia to India. The whole peninsula of India was peopled by a race of this character before the influx of Arians. (p. 650)

Additionally, precolonial military history provides additional evidence for Africa and Asia's connections, and much of this history stems from the pharaonic periods (Mokhtar, 1981).

In sum, there is a line of historical inquiry that suggests the Egyptians conquered over 110 foreign states in the 16th century B.C.E. (Diop, 1981b), including many in the Mediterranean and western Asia. These regions and countries include Crete (modern-day Greece), Cyprus (Mediterranean), Cyclades (southeast of mainland Greece), Mitani (modern-day Turkey), Kadesh, Syria, and Babylonia (Breasted, 1930). While detailed military history expands beyond the scope of this book, it is important to highlight that precolonial Africans were avid travelers with geographical, military, and maritime acumen.

Social studies theme (2) time, continuity, and change, suggests that social studies programs should include experiences that provide for the study of the past and its legacy. These findings align with this and social studies theme (3) people, places, and environment, which contributes to understanding the relationship between human populations and the physical world. For example, Figure 6.3 shows Gudea of Lagash, a ruler whose religious texts and statues provide significant evidence of his rulership and reign. The area of his governance is now known as southeastern Iraq.

Over 30 statues and artifacts of Gudea are on display in museums around the world as testaments to his role in the Akkadian Empire. According to Edzard (1997), the inscription on his robe can be translated as follows:

> When Ningirsu, the mighty warrior of Enlil, had established a courtyard in the city for Ningišzida, son of Ninazu, the beloved one among the gods; when he had established for him irrigated plots(?) on the agricultural land; (and) when Gudea, ruler of Lagaš, the straightforward one, beloved by his (personal) god, had built the Eninnu, the White Thunderbird, and the . . . , his "heptagon," for Ningirsu, his lord, (then) for Nanše, the powerful lady, his lady, did he build the Sirara House. . . . He (also) built the individual houses of (other) great gods of Lagaš. For Ningišzida, his (personal) god, he built his House of Girsu. Someone (in the future) whom Ningirsu, his god—as my god (addressed me)—has (directly) addressed within the crowd, let him not, thereafter, be envious(?) with regard to the house of my (personal) god. Let him invoke its (the house's) name; let such a person be my friend, and let him (also) invoke my (own) name. (Gudea) fashioned a statue of himself. "Let the life of Gudea, who built the house, be long."—(this is how) he named (the statue) for his sake, and he brought it to him into (his) house. (pp. 57–58)

This passage further illustrates the importance of Gudea of Lagash in world history. To support the unbleaching process, teaching about this in world history aligns with the following NCSS themes: (1) culture; (2) time, continuity, and change; (3) people, places, and environments; (6) power, authority, and governance; and (9) global connections. Including the experiences of Gudea in the curriculum thus provides a background for discussing cultural diversity within the context of past legacies, people, places, and environments. Gudea was a leader whose power, authority, and governance contextualize

Figure 6.3. Gudea of Lagash, ca. 1250 B.C.E. (Source: Wikicommons)

how people create, interact with, and change such systems. These artifacts are from the Neo-Sumerian period dating circa 2090 B.C.E. in Mesopotamia.

An unbleached curriculum unit on Gudea might explore how political power operates, as well as the purposes and roles of government. Students can also make connections between the global connections during this early time frame and the contemporary period. For instance, the curriculum can address the influence of global interdependence on patterns of international migration. Similarly, the Dancing Girl of the Mohenjo-Daro (meaning "Mound of the Dead Men") was found in an archaeological site in the province of Sindh, Pakistan (see Figure 6.4). One of the largest settlements of the ancient Indus Valley civilization, the Mohenjo-Daro dates circa 2500 B.C.E.

According to NCSS theme (9) global connections, social studies programs should include experiences that provide for the study of global connections and interdependence. In the case of the Indus Valley civilization, the question of what is needed for life to thrive on an ever-changing and increasingly interdependent planet can be explored, as well as how global connections have existed in the past, how they exist currently, and how they are likely to exist in the future. This is important for learners in U.S. public schools because it provides the context for the discussion of the origins of civilizations and the movement of people around the world.

In the case of the African presence in Cambodia, significant evidence remains in the 200 stone faces at Bayon that are on display for the world to witness (Chatterji, 1939). Bayon, a Cambodian Buddhist pyramid temple in Angkor Thom, represented the symbolic center of the Kher Empire. Angkor Thom was built by King Jayavarman VII (Sharrock, 2013; Shelby, 1998). The four face pillars were excavated after much of Bayon was ruined (Chatterji, 1939). Over 200 stone carvings remain as evidence of the African influence in Cambodia. These findings may also support Herodotus's and Diodorus's earlier treatises.

Similarly, the African influence in Turkey is also very important for expanding the curriculum to prevent bleaching and whitewashing. Evidence of an African presence in Turkey is featured in museums around the world. As supported in the historical accounts of Diodorus and Herodotus, African people have influenced world history in multiple places around the globe. NCSS theme (9) global connections, aligns with this in curriculum development.

As in Turkey, the African presence is also demonstrated in Etruscan civilization, an area in modern-day Italy between the Tiber and Arno Rivers west and south of the Apennines. The head of an African youth dated circa 375 B.C.E. prominently displays African features. Another example of African influence is the head of an African youth dating circa 330 B.C.E., which is displayed in the Virginia Museum of Fine Arts (Rusak, 1996).

Figure 6.4. Dancing Girl, Mohenjo-Daro—Art from the Indus Valley Civilization. (Source: Wikicommons)

These artifacts comprise the collections of the world's major museums due to their importance in documenting the interconnections of world populations over time. Artifacts speak directly to Herodotus's and Diodorus's observations. The preservation of these artifacts reflects the civilizations they represent. As noted in NCSS themes 1, 2, 3, 5, and 9, the importance of culture and global interdependence can help correct a bleached and whitewashed curriculum by shedding light on African contributions in Asia and Europe.

The African influence on world religions is revelatory in the rise of Zen Buddhism and the Moors and the spread of Islam. The founder of Zen Buddhism was believed to be of African descent (Diop, 1989; Suzuki, 1960, 1991). The African influence in major world religions is well documented (Diop, 1974; Drake, 1987; Mbiti, 2015). In addition to Buddhism, the Moorish influence on Islam is well established. Next, we explore the Moors and their African influence in Spain. For more detailed discussion on the African presence in Asia, see Runoko Rashidi's *African Star over Asia: The Black Presence in the East* (Rashidi, 2012) and *Black Star: The African Presence in Early Europe* (Rashidi, 2011).

UNBLEACHING AND THE MOORS IN EUROPE

According to recent archaeology and scholarship, the Moors flourished in Al-Andalus of the Iberian Peninsula in the region of Spain and Portugal (Southwest Europe) for more than 700 years—from 711 C.E. until 1492 (Lane-Poole, 1893; Pimienta-Bey, 1992, 2002). Due to the proximity of the Rock of Gibraltar in southern Spain to the tip of Morocco in North Africa, in the ancient world there were regular travels, trades, and interactions between Africans and Europeans, as the two continents (North Africa and southern Europe are bordering regions) are so close to each other. Even today, the trip back and forth across the Mediterranean Sea into Europe and back to Africa is a popular travel excursion.

For example, in a description of the Moors, Manilius's *Astronomica* (40 C.E./1977) explains the voyages of the Africans. Manilius notes:

> The Ethiopians stain the world and depict a race of men steeped in darkness; less sun-burnt are the natives of India; the land of Egypt, flooded by the Nile, darkens bodies more mildly owing to the inundation of its fields: it is a country nearer to us and its moderate climate imparts a medium tone. . . . The Moors derive their name from their faces, and their identity is proclaimed by the colour of their skins. (p. 281)

This fact helps to underscore Herodotus's and Diodorus's earlier findings on the Black presence in Asia. Due to the close proximity of the two regions, North Africa and southern Europe, there have been many cultural exchanges. Historically, the Moorish advances in mathematics, astronomy, art, and agriculture helped propel Europe out of the Dark Ages and into the Renaissance (Pimienta-Bey, 1992).

According to Blakemore (2019), in 711 C.E., a group of North African Muslims led by the Berber general Tariq ibn-Ziyad captured the Iberian Peninsula (modern Spain and Portugal). Known as Al-Andalus, the territory became a prosperous cultural and economic center where education and the arts and sciences flourished. NCSS theme (1) culture, notes that social studies programs should include experiences that provide for the study of culture. Studying the Moors and their contributions can expand the curriculum to explore how cultural diffusion occurs within and across communities, regions, and nations.

Similarly, theme (2) time, continuity, and change, notes that social studies programs should include experiences that provide for the study of the past and its legacy. In today's world, social, cultural, economic, and civic issues demand that students apply knowledge, skills, and understandings to appreciate how people interact with the environment and what some of the consequences are of those interactions. The Moors and their influence in Spain as well as the contributions of Africans in European and Asian history support the need for an unbleaching of the curriculum.

To create a more just and humane society, unbleaching seeks to foster greater inclusion by analyzing, critiquing, and disrupting systems of oppression that universalize the interests of one group over all others. Each generation has a responsibility to the next to help create a better future and to help mitigate injustice and pain and suffering. Unbleaching embraces the promise of a society that addresses the needs of future generations and their right to live in a world that promotes social justice and educational equity and excellence for all students.

CHAPTER SUMMARY

This chapter addressed the importance of unbleaching as a corrective to the whitewashed curriculum in use in U.S. public schools. It featured the contributions of Africans to European and Asian history by centering the work of historians Diodorus and Herodotus. Furthermore, this chapter places these omissions in the context of U.S. social studies curricula. In the next chapter we discuss the overall implications and policy recommendations of unbleaching the curriculum in U.S. schools.

Chapter 7

Unbleaching

Contemporary Issues in Curriculum Design and Instruction

> *To control a people you must first control what they think about themselves and how they regard their history and culture. And when your conqueror makes you ashamed of your culture and your history, he needs no prison walls and no chains to hold you.*
>
> —*John Henrik Clarke*

In the previous chapter, we discussed the African or Black presence in Europe and Asia. In this final chapter, we investigate how unbleaching the curriculum can help mitigate the effects of hegemonic curricula that perpetuate harmful practices against minority students. This chapter discusses education reform, curriculum design, and teacher pedagogy.

In U.S. public schools, the effects of a hegemonic curriculum generally include omissions (PtahHotep and Imhotep), suppressed contributions (Olmec), falsifications (the Ahmes Papyrus renamed the Rhind Manuscript), whitening up history, and whitewashing the curriculum. As we discussed earlier in this book, the generally low student achievement in the U.S., ongoing miseducation, and teacher shortage speak to the need for educational change (Adichie, 2009; Byford & Russell, 2007; Ighodaro & Wiggan, 2011; Watson-Vandiver & Wiggan, 2020; Woodson, 1933/2006). As such, a corrected curriculum that is unbleached can help yield improved student learning outcomes. Notwithstanding the prospects of improving U.S. school achievement, correcting the curriculum to address miseducation and falsifications is the right thing to do for all students. Additionally, culturally responsive pedagogy that focuses on educational processes that are humane and democratic and that mitigate curriculum violence can contribute to enhanced student outcomes (Akua, 2020; Banks, 2010; Gay, 2018; Ighodaro & Wiggan, 2011; Ladson-Billings, 1998, 2003; Watson-Vandiver & Wiggan, 2018).

Related to the themes of this book and the importance of systematically unbleaching the curriculum, bell hooks (2014) highlights an important point to consider:

> Some folks think that everyone who supports cultural diversity wants to replace one dictatorship of knowing with another, changing one set way of thinking for another. This is perhaps the gravest misperception of cultural diversity. (p. 32)

In light of hooks's (2014) treatise, those who oppose inclusion may generally make false claims of reverse discrimination. This is often an easy pass for those who may feel threatened by DEI work, which they may view as challenging their power or privilege or as a basis of manufacturing blame or guilt. Notwithstanding some forms of hesitance, there is an urgent need to provide a corrected curriculum, one that focuses on historical accuracy. To that end, the premise of unbleaching is to center curricula and pedagogy on historical facts. For example, by repositioning Africa to its rightful place as the birthplace of humanity (National Human Genome Institute, 2006/2011; Smedley & Smedley, 2005), unbleaching promotes greater historical and anthropological accuracy for all learners. Unbleaching is not an issue for minority students; rather, the inclusion of curricular omissions is beneficial for all—teachers and students alike—as it enhances and expands instructional knowledge and learning.

In the U.S., schools are generally modeled after the larger society and are thereby impacted by racism and socioeconomic inequities that reflect the interests of the dominant group (Artiles & Trent, 2016). As such, curriculum standards govern what is taught in U.S. schools and can be impacted by ideological distortions that perpetuate institutionalized racism. Thus, there is a great need for curriculum reform that addresses the ways master-scripting promotes a "single story" (Adichie, 2009; NCSS, 2018).

As mentioned earlier in this book, the single story begins at some point other than the beginning and shows a people as only one thing (Adichie, 2009). In this case, Africa is the origin of the human family tree and civilization (National Human Genome Institute, 2006/2011; Smedley & Smedley, 2005). And as such, the curriculum must be corrected to reflect this fact. The single story does not provide an accurate account of the multiple perspectives that inform human history, but instead presents an often one-sided White supremacist view that becomes the guiding narrative. In light of the single story, there have been many legal challenges to educational inequities— *United States & Ridley v. State of Georgia (Coweta)* [2006]; *Fisher & United States v. Tucson Unified School District* [2013]; *Cowan & United States v.*

Bolivar County Board of Education No. 4 [2017] (Cleveland School District, Mississippi)—which supports our treatise on the need for unbleaching education processes and practices (Teasdell & Wiggan, 2022).

UNBLEACHING AND OUR HUMAN RESPONSIBILITY

Today's political climate is notably divisive (Leatherby et al., 2021; Simon & Sidner, 2021). Thus, the work of unbleaching is needed for all of us. In this sense, we all have a responsibility to help make schools and society become more humane and just. This is something that each generation must help ensure for the next. Our survival as members of the human family tree depends on this. However, one of the key issues in the U.S. is the complexities and sensitivities surrounding the nation's history and issues of racial and ethnic relations. Moreover, attacks on critical race theory (CRT) and the 1619 Project, as well as racist attempts to deny Pulitzer Prize–winning reporter Nikole Hannah-Jones tenure, indicate that there are major challenges (Hannah-Jones, 2021; Jeong, 2021; Lang, 2020; Vaughan, 2021).

In the context of unbleaching, the 1619 Project sheds light on the ways in which history is silenced or suppressed and how those who reveal or speak truth are villainized. While racism in the U.S. is often positioned as a partisan "conservative" issue, the fact remains that the divisions in the country have been generally bipartisan. To this point, in 2021, Senator Raphael Warnock, the first elected Black senator from Georgia since Reconstruction, explained in his speech on the congressional floor:

> Here's the thing we must remember: Slavery was bipartisan. Jim Crow segregation was bipartisan. The refusal of women's suffrage was bipartisan. The denial of the basic dignity of members of the LGBTQ community has long been bipartisan. The three-fifths compromise was the creation of a putative, national unity at the expense of Black people's basic humanity. (J. Jones, 2021)

In regard to Senator Warnock's speech, much of today's scapegoating and blaming has less to do with social progress and issues of equity. As such, it is important to consider the comprehensive history of race relations and discrimination in the U.S.

The subjugation of women, minorities, and LGBTQ+ individuals has been long standing. This connects to how we must address educational issues today. The need for unbleaching and antiracism work is crucial in public schools (S. D. Dei, 1996; Kendi, 2019). Thus, it is a bipartisan responsibility to address educational inequity in schools, starting with the curriculum. Truth is a human project, not a political one. This further highlights the importance of unbleaching, which aims to remove the harmful effects of curriculum violence to instead promote accuracy and truth. This work requires collaboration among all stakeholders to better understand the intersections of race, power, and privilege.

Historically, there have been many legal challenges that support the need for unbleaching the curriculum. Unfortunately, many of these issues are still unresolved today. The *Brown v. Board of Education* (1954) decision attempted to ensure greater equity through court-mandated desegregation, yet research indicates that schools are more divided in the 21st century than they were in the 1950s (Chapman, 2008; Gaillard, 2006; Magness & Page, 2011; Richmond, 2012). Thus, even though *Brown v. Board of Education* (1954) legally outlawed de jure segregation, the nation has been challenged with providing equal access to educational opportunities for African Americans in particular.

The Dream Long Deferred: The Landmark Struggle for Desegregation in Charlotte, North Carolina describes the effects of segregation in public schools (Gaillard, 2006). The book explains the 1971 *Swann vs. Charlotte Mecklenburg Schools* case and the attempts at blocking desegregation. While there has been some progress, public schools remain highly segregated (Donnor & Dixson, 2013; Orfield & Yun, 1999). Parental social class continues to be a basis of neighborhood processes. And school funding disparities generally place minority students in lower-quality schools with disproportionate special education placement and instruction from less qualified teachers. This has compounding effects on students' educational trajectories. In fact, Kunjufu (2020) asserts that two consecutive years of having an ineffective teacher or nonrigorous learning can undermine a child's educational trajectory. Thus, this book examines the role of unbleaching the curriculum in mediating racialization and marginalization of minority contributions. A bleached curriculum limits students' access to high-quality education and rigor. In this regard, the power of unbleaching proves timely.

Given the effects of the COVID-19 pandemic, there is a need for highly qualified teachers to address the pronounced learning loss particularly among underserved students (Donnelly & Patrinos, 2021; Dorn et al., 2020). In "Breaking the Legacy of Teacher Shortages," Darling-Hammond (2022) asserts that there is a need for a comprehensive plan to revitalize the teaching profession and support teachers. The pandemic learning loss and the teacher shortage are just two aspects of the problems with today's public schools (Donnelly & Patrinos, 2021; Dorn et al., 2020; Garcia & Weiss, 2020). Thus, it is imperative to upend inequitable educational policies to ensure that all students are taught from a curriculum that reflects truth, rigor, and high quality.

As a background to this problem, Anderson's (1988) *The Education of Blacks in the South* illustrates how, from its beginnings, the American educational system was not designed to educate all children toward their fullest potential. Similarly, in *The White Architects of Black Education: Ideology and Power in America, 1865–1954*, Watkins (2001) explains the social and historical context of the White power brokers who were shaping Black education for their own personal gain. In light of the prevalence of White privilege, these architects designed a curriculum that not only bleached history but also served to protect privilege while othering and suppressing minoritized groups (Watkins, 2001). The White architects subsequently whitewashed the curriculum, hence the need for unbleaching.

Still today, for minoritized students in U.S. schools, access to an unbleached curriculum and culturally responsive pedagogical practices present ongoing challenges (Delpit, 2006, 2019; Gay, 2018; Ladson-Billings & Tate, 1995; Paris & Alim, 2017; Watson-Vandiver & Wiggan, 2020). Cases such as *United States & Ridley v. State of Georgia (Coweta)* (2006); *Fisher & United States v. Tucson Unified School District* (2013); *Cowan & United States v. Bolivar County Board of Education No. 4* (2017) (Cleveland School District, Mississippi) provide examples of how the U.S. education system is challenged by inequities in student treatment and teacher preparation (Teasdell & Wiggan, 2022). Thus, there is a great need for school reform and policy change.

According to the Office of Civil Rights and the U.S. Department of Education, approximately 1,100 lawsuits addressing racialized inequities are currently pending (U.S. Department of Education, 2021). For example, legal cases such as *Milwaukee Public Schools* and *Tucson Unified School District* have provided pathways to educational reform (Hansen et al., 2018). The 2021 veto of the Ensuring Dignity & Nondiscrimination/Schools legislation known as House Bill 324 (HB 324) in North Carolina (and 27 other states) has intensified conversations surrounding race, CRT, and its recent extension in critical race structuralism (CRS) (Wiggan et al., 2020). As we mentioned before, HB 324 was designed to prohibit teaching or presenting evidence regarding disparities in racial and ethnic relations and gaps in the treatment of minoritized groups (Pitkin, 2021). In this sense, there are many attempts at silencing meaningful teaching and lesson planning surrounding racial and ethnic relations, and other social issues.

To mediate the challenges noted above, legal action has initiated curriculum reform efforts in several states. For example, in New Jersey, with the passage of the 2002 Amistad Bill, the state became one of the first in the U.S. to make Black history a part of the core curriculum (Baptiste, 2010). Following suit, in 2005, Philadelphia mandated Black history as a graduation requirement for high school students (Broderick, 2014). In 2020, the Texas State Board of Education approved the creation of a statewide African American Studies course (Grisby, 2020). Similarly, Illinois requires public colleges and universities to offer Black history courses (L. J. King, 2017). After over a decade of development and requests for adoption, in 2022, the College Board approved its first Advanced Placement (AP) African American Studies course (Hartocollis, 2022; Waxman, 2022).

In spite of these gains, U.S. public schools still face many barriers in racial equity (Hansen et al., 2018; Reardon et al., 2012). Debate over the teaching of CRT and the 1619 Project in public schools have undermined some aspects of needed curricular change (Hannah-Jones, 2021; Ladson-Billings & Tate, 1998; Lang, 2020). Furthermore, at least 19 states have passed legislation to regulate how race is discussed in schools (Waxman, 2022). In this sense, the curriculum is viewed as a place of contested power, where those who are at the table and making the decisions can speak to the interests of some stakeholders while omitting the contributions and perspectives of others. Thus, to mitigate the effects of curriculum violence, there is a need to unbleach the curriculum to include suppressed contributions.

Given these issues, the practice of unbleaching the curriculum is crucial. As noted, in the context of this book, unbleaching is the process of disrupting Eurocentrism and systems of oppression that undermine, suppress, falsify, dehumanize, and marginalize non-Europeans and their perspectives and contributions as conduits for creating and maintaining power and privilege. Here, we reemphasize the tenets and principles of unbleaching to provide a guiding framework for our closing discussion. In chapter 1, we defined *unbleaching* as the systemic and institutional work that disrupts Eurocentrism and hegemonic master-scripting that positions and transmits a dominant group's (Whites') interests. In this way, multicultural perspectives and DEI are central to the related purpose of all educational work inclusive of hiring, professional development, retention, promotion, leadership, curriculum development, lesson planning, instruction, assessment, student treatment, etc.

Unbleaching focuses on dismantling exclusionary practices and therefore does not just supplement already racist institutional processes and systems regarding education, school, and curriculum design. Instead, unbleaching brings diverse perspectives and multiculturalism in school and curriculum development. As part of a critical and reflective process, unbleaching analyzes the ways in which the interests of the dominant group have been positioned as the basis of—and as the standard for human achievement, aesthetics, intelligence, and curricular and instructional design—at the expense of non-White perspectives and contributions. In the context of education, unbleaching embeds DEI as core tenets of educational change, particularly in curriculum development, lesson planning, teacher pedagogy, school leadership, and student assessment. Again, unbleaching is not anti-White or anti-European; rather, it is a purposeful process intended to dismantle systems of racial oppression, as well as falsification and omission surrounding minoritized people's contributions and perspectives.

UNBLEACHING AND SOCIAL STUDIES CURRICULUM REDESIGN

A key tenet of unbleaching is the principle of human responsibility and interconnectedness. Science has proven that all humans share 99.9% of the same DNA (Shared DNA, 2005). As we noted, the mapping of the Human Genome Project shows that the 3 billion DNA base pairs of human beings are shared by all humans (National Human Genome Institute, 2006/2011; Smedley & Smedley, 2005). This suggests that we are more similar than different and that all 8 billion people who inhabit planet earth are indeed of African descent (United Nations, 2022). Thus, anthropology, archaeology, and science have provided evidence that East Africa—Ethiopia—is the birthplace of humanity (National Human Genome Institute, 2006/2011; Shared DNA, 2005; Smedley & Smedley, 2005). This suggests that 0.1% of human DNA explains differences in phenotype, which are falsely constructed as *race* or as differences in races. Indeed, since all humans share 99.9% of the same DNA, they belong to the same family tree (National Human Genome Institute, 2006/2011; Shared DNA, 2005; Smedley & Smedley, 2005).

As noted, Africa is the place of the first written language, MDW-NTR (pronounced "meh-doo neh-ter"—later called hieroglyphics); the oldest books in the world; and the multi-genius Imhotep, who wrote the world's first medical papyrus (the Imhotep Medical Papyrus, 2267 B.C.E.—later purchased and renamed the Edwin Smith Papyrus, 1862 C.E.). Due to whitewashing, the Ahmes Manuscript is now called the Rhind Manuscript. Yet it is the oldest mathematical document in the world. However, this information is often omitted or marginalized in the curriculum. Similarly, *The Teachings of PtahHotep* (2300 B.C.E.) is regarded as the oldest book in the world and *The Book of the Coming Forth by Day* (2200 B.C.E.) as the world's first religious book. Yet there is silence on these contributions in the curriculum and in NCSS standards.

These works necessitate appropriate positioning in curriculum design to provide a more inclusive and complete picture of humanity. The contributions of the Olmec as the oldest civilization in the Americas are largely suppressed in school curricula. This is true for K–12 public schools and higher education, which are generally imbued in Eurocentrism. Thus, unbleaching upends Eurocentrism by disrupting the myth of White supremacy and allows us to see our common humanity, rather than emphasizing differences as a basis of marginalizing and discriminating against others as a source of exacting power and privilege. Unbleaching can help to unpack bias, which is common among all humans, and raise awareness and build inclusive practices that mitigate against racism, ethnocentrism, and Eurocentrism in schools and beyond. Social studies should reflect this principle and its alignment with its standards for global connections if it is to reach its highest potential and more directly address DEI (NCSS, 2017).

For curriculum designers and in light of social studies, educators must be reminded that "dysconscious racism" is an uncritical habit of mind—involving attitudes, assumptions, and beliefs—that results in the justification of inequity and exploitation, which leads to acceptance of the existing order (J. E. King, 1991). As noted previously, dysconsciousness, then, can be unintentionally reflected in curricular and education design that distorts or suppresses non-White contributions (J. E. King, 1991). Thus, unbleaching is a purposeful response to "dysconscious racism" and curriculum violence.

Generally in the U.S., those who hold political and economic power control the curriculum as a reflection of that power. Thus, the curriculum tells us who is important and what is worth knowing as an extension of a dominant group. For over 10 years, the College Board has initiated efforts to include Black history and teaching about early African contributions in AP-level courses. In 2022, the approval and introduction of this AP African American Studies course marked a great step in the direction toward DEI (Hartocollis, 2022; Waxman, 2022). Yet, more reform is needed.

UNBLEACHING AND FEDERAL SCHOOL REFORM

In the parlance of public schools, unbleaching the curriculum is directly connected to the need for school reform and to the generally modest performance scores (NAEP, 2022a, 2022b), as well as to the need for more DEI work. Policies such as No Child Left Behind (2002), the Every Student Succeeds Act (2015), and other federal school reform efforts have greatly impacted teaching practices and student outcomes (Hansen et al., 2018; U.S. Commission on Civil Rights, 2010). As we have noted, the fourth- and eighth-grade scores in reading and mathematics across the board reveal performance below NAEP proficiency standards. According to *The Nation's Report Card*, on a scale of 0–500, trends in fourth-grade NAEP average reading scores ranged from 215 in 1992 to 217 in 2022 (NAEP, 2022a). Furthermore, as we noted, in eighth-grade reading, only 31% of students were at or above proficiency, and 69% were below proficiency (NAEP, 2022b). On the same report card for eighth grade, NAEP average reading scores ranged below proficiency, remaining at 260 in both 1992 and 2022 (NAEP, 2022a).

There are similar underperformance data trends in mathematics (NAEP, 2022b). On a scale of 0–500, fourth- and eighth-grade NAEP scores in mathematics have remained below proficiency from 1990 to 2019 (NAEP, 2022a, 2022b). Average fourth-grade NAEP mathematics scores declined by five points from 241 in 2019 to 236 in 2022. Similarly, in eighth grade, NAEP average mathematics scores ranged below proficiency from 263 in 1990 to 274 in 2022. This is an eight-point decrease since 2019 (NAEP, 2022a, 2022b). Moreover, only 26% of eighth graders performed at or above proficiency in mathematics, and 74% did not (NAEP, 2022a).

As a result of the COVID-19 pandemic, there was a further decrease in student scores (NAEP, 2022a, 2022b). The COVID-19 pandemic impacted learning worldwide due to the need for students to move from face-to-face instruction to virtual learning. This particularly affected low socioeconomic students who may have experienced limited access to technology and parental support at home. From a curricular and pedagogical perspective, the decrease in student scores tells a much more complicated story about what is happening in U.S. schools. The general underperformance reflects a need for effective school reform.

Federal reform in U.S. schools has undergone significant movement in the last few decades as each president sought to find solutions to pervasive educational challenges. Enacted by the 107th U.S. Congress under the leadership of President George W. Bush (2001–2009), the No Child Left Behind (NCLB) Act of 2001 reauthorized the 1965 Elementary and Secondary Education Act (ESEA) (Bush, 2001). It included Title I provisions for poor students to improve their academic progress. The NCLB Act's stated aim was to leave no child behind by closing the achievement (opportunity) gap with accountability, flexibility, and choice. The goal was for every student in every school to be proficient in reading and mathematics.

Notwithstanding stated good intentions, redesign efforts that do not take into account the complexity of school systems and areas that require reform (culturally responsive teaching and leading, school discipline disparities, dropout prevention, and disproportionality in special education) can in fact perpetuate harmful practices. With NCLB, the emphasis on testing led to compromised pedagogical practices and "failing" schools. Revisions to NCLB also indicated a continuing trend toward "teaching to the test" to reach established standards. While NCLB created measures that exposed achievement (opportunity) gaps among traditionally underserved students and their peers, it also prompted debates on education improvement.

With the election of President Barack Obama (2009–2017), the first Black president of the U.S., considerable attention was directed toward revising and rewriting the NCLB version of the 1965 Elementary and Secondary Education Act (Standerfer, 2006). President Obama's NCLB version 2.0 led to an expansion of the Race to the Top initiative, an increase in college access with improved federal financing options, and strengthened STEM education through teacher preparation (McGuinn, 2012). Due to a number of political impediments, NCLB 2.0 was not successfully implemented (Dee et al., 2013; Lee & Reeves, 2012).

In December 2015, President Obama signed the Every Student Succeeds Act (ESSA) as the reauthorization of ESEA. To promote equal opportunity for all students, ESSA aimed to fully prepare students for success in college and careers through multiple paths (McGuinn, 2016). First, ESSA advanced equity by upholding critical protections for America's disadvantaged and high-need students. ESSA emphasized high standards that promote college readiness and access to high-quality preschool (Sharp, 2016). While ESSA improved on NCLB and advanced the ESEA established by President Lyndon Johnson in 1965, additional reform efforts were initiated with the election of new political leaders (Standerfer, 2006).

Under the Donald Trump administration (2017–2021), Secretary of Education Betsy DeVos advocated for school choice and gave states the power to implement the ESSA (Thompson et al., 2020; Wong, 2020). This led to defunding Title I support and other specific allocations aimed at helping underserved schools. Public schools saw some of the greatest cuts in funding as privatization models were being emphasized. Under this presidency, some of the gains made by previous administrations were regressed. During the COVID-19 pandemic, both Trump and DeVos advocated for return to in-person instruction and funded community service block grants for scholarships to families to promote access to in-person learning.

The election of President Joseph Biden (2021–present) and the first Black woman vice president, Kamala Harris, also represented shifts in federal education reform. Under the Build Back Better effort and the American Rescue Plan, Biden addressed the ongoing challenges to education due to the COVID-19 pandemic. His administration also attempted to address intergenerational educational disparities and the need for stronger and more equitable schools. In 2021, Biden appointed Secretary of Education Miguel Cardona whose focus is on eliminating long-standing inequities and closing racial and socioeconomic opportunity gaps while expanding access to higher education. Notwithstanding the attempts at reforms noted above, U.S. schools are still experiencing underperformance and gaps in the treatment of students, where Black and Brown students are most negatively impacted.

As such, the curriculum is one important place where change must begin. In this sense, unbleaching can hold promise for federal school reform. There should be parity in how students learn about human contributions, and this should focus on DEI. Curricular redesign and culturally responsive practices have the potential to improve student outcomes and teacher preparation

(Durden, 2008; Gay, 2018; Ladson-Billings, 2016). This is particularly important as U.S. student demographics continue to change and become more diverse.

UNBLEACHING AND TEACHING PREPARATION PROGRAMS

Based on the U.S. Census Bureau report and other government data, by the year 2060, minority students are projected to represent 64% of U.S. public school student enrollment (NCES, 2020; U.S. Census, 2015). In fact, as noted, according to the U.S. Census, the multiracial population has increased by 276% from 9 million people in 2010 to 33.8 million people in 2020, and it will continue to increase by 226% over the next 40 years (U.S. Census, 2015, 2020). Notwithstanding, White teachers represent 79% of the public school teacher workforce and have consistently been near the 80th percentile over the last five decades (NCES, 2020). Additionally, the U.S. educational system is challenged by inequities in quality schools and disparities in the treatment of students, and many teachers are entering the field underprepared to teach minority learners (Acosta et al., 2018; Asante, 2017; Darling-Hammond, 2007; Darling-Hammond et al., 2017). Despite changing student demographics, the teaching numbers are expected to remain relatively constant (NCES, 2020). As such, there is a great need for addressing the teacher shortage, as well as to improve teacher preparation to better address the needs of the nation's diverse learners. Toward this end, correcting the curriculum and transforming teaching practices can promote DEI and greater inclusion and help improve student achievement.

In the purview of unbleaching, teacher hiring practices and preservice teacher education are crucial areas that need attention (Freire, 1970/2018; hooks, 2014). In fact, classroom instruction is a central place where whitewashing and bleaching occur (Akbar, 1998). To this issue, hooks (2014) describes how transformative education must also include a change in classroom teaching. hooks (2014) notes:

> The call for a recognition of cultural diversity, a rethinking of ways of knowing, a deconstruction of old epistemologies, and the concomitant demand that there be a transformation in our classrooms, in how we teach and what we teach, has been a necessary revolution—one that seeks to restore life to a corrupt and dying academy. (p. 30)

In relation to classroom pedagogy and the work of unbleaching teaching practices, research consistently shows that two consecutive years of poor teaching can irreversibly affect students' learning outcomes (Kunjufu, 2020). Additionally, studies also contend that students learn best in diverse learning environments (Figlio, 2017; Gershenson et al., 2021; Gurin et al., 2002). This demonstrates a need to further explore the ways in which teachers are recruited and hired in relation to the students they serve. Some of these studies are discussed in greater detail below.

In "Diversity and Higher Education: Theory and Impact on Educational Outcomes," Gurin et al. (2002) finds that greater classroom diversity led to positive educational interactions among racially and ethnically diverse groups. Some of the positive learning outcomes observed in the study included increased student motivation and engagement, stronger critical thinking, improved problem-solving skills, and increased student writing skills (Gurin et al., 2002). Additionally, a National Bureau of Economic Research study (Gershenson et al., 2021) shows that diverse teacher representation has a positive impact on K–12 students' learning. Some of the benefits of increased teacher diversity include diversity of thought, helping students understand—and confront—racism, preparing students to live in a multicultural society, and fostering fewer interactions of cultural bias. These same benefits of diverse teacher representation are also supported by the Brookings Institute (Figlio, 2017) and the Center for American Progress (Boser, 2011).

In addition to behavioral and interpersonal benefits, a 2021 National Bureau of Economic Research study also finds that teacher diversity leads to improved student performance (Gershenson et al., 2021). The findings suggest that students who experienced a diverse teacher workforce had better academic performance and increased likelihood of attending college or university (Gershenson et al., 2021). More specifically, Gershenson et al. (2021) found that having one teacher of color yielded a 13% increase in student attendance, and two teachers of color resulted in a 32% increase. While race is not indicative of effective teaching, these findings suggest that more DEI work is needed.

Given the data noted above, there is a need for greater teacher diversity, as well as inclusive pedagogical practices and a comprehensive redesign of the curriculum. However, today's public school education is challenged by systemic racism, especially in relation to recent attacks on CRT and the very notion of mentioning the country's troubled past and present in the classroom (Lang, 2020; Perez & Guadiano, 2020; Romero, 2010). As such, unbleaching attempts to provide greater DEI work in education. Much like the victory in the *Brown v. Board of Education* (1954) case, which declared segregated schools to be unconstitutional, curricula should also be racially inclusive for all students. In this regard, unbleaching asserts that separate curricula, via additive holidays and celebratory months, are not enough and does not address equity and inclusion in order to create deep systemic change.

There are critical needs in education reform, specifically in regard to addressing miseducation and curriculum violence. While Loewen's (2008) *Lies My Teacher Told Me*, Zinn and Stefoff's (2009) *Young People's History*, Ighodaro and Wiggan's (2011) *Curriculum Violence: America's New Civil Rights Issue*, and other well-known critical works attempt to add missing content, more change is needed to advance greater DEI in curricula and assessment. This is particularly appropriate given the testing climate in contemporary U.S. schools. In light of unbleaching, there is a need to mitigate the compounding effects of high-stakes assessments practices (Darling-Hammond et al., 2017), rote learning, drills, and memorization, which have supplanted educational rigor and critical thinking. Compounding the high-stakes testing climate, many schools have also silenced discussions on race to avoid controversy (Crouch, 2014; A. Johnson, 2018; Lang, 2020). This is often done to protect White supremacy and fragility.

Research consistently illustrates that there are academic and social benefits to antiracist education (S. D. Dei, 1996; Kendi, 2019), especially in relation to providing counternarratives and centering minority contributions (J. E. King & Swartz, 2018; Watson-Vandiver & Wiggan, 2020). Thus, with the recent resurgence of hate crimes (Huerta, 2020; Human Rights Watch, 2020), racial violence (Murphy, 2020), and political divisions (Leatherby et al., 2021; Simon & Sidner, 2021), schools should not force silence, as these are issues that are relevant to students' lives. As such, this book reimagines the possibilities for schools and society where greater inclusion can help foster positive social change. Thus, unbleaching is the systemic and institutional work that disrupts Eurocentrism and hegemony. In doing so, unbleaching consistently challenges suppression, omission, and falsification in the curriculum and beyond.

UNBLEACHING AND DEI

In regard to school curricula, unbleaching helps to upend curriculum violence and whitewashing in education to centrally place DEI in all school processes. In *Teaching to Transgress*, hooks (2014) explains that the constant process of learning and relearning is an integral part of transformative education. Additionally, hooks (2014) notes that the art of teaching to transgress and infusing multiculturalism helps educators disrupt various forms of hegemony. hooks (2014) notes:

> Multiculturalism compels educators to recognize the narrow boundaries that have shaped the way knowledge is shared in the classroom. It forces us all to recognize our complicity in accepting and perpetuating biases of any kind.

> Students are eager to break through barriers to knowing. They are willing to surrender to the wonder of re-learning and learning ways of knowing that go against the grain. When we, as educators, allow our pedagogy to be radically changed by our recognition of a multicultural world, we can give students the education they desire and deserve. We can teach in ways that transform consciousness, creating a climate of free expression that is the essence of a truly liberatory liberal arts education. (p. 44)

Given hooks's (2014) argument for multicultural education, educators must become more responsive to the academic and social needs of their students.

With the emergence of the COVID-19 health crisis (March 2020), the U.S. also witnessed significant social unrest, such as the publicly televised murder of George Floyd and the unlawful killings of Breonna Taylor, Ahmaud Arbery, and many others at the hands of the police. On January 6, 2021, in a deliberate show of White privilege and racism, a band of riotous civilians, at the alleged urging of then-president Donald Trump, besieged the U.S. Capitol and raided government offices (Leatherby et al., 2021). This unprecedented uprising against President Joseph Biden's administration (2021–present) and the first Black female vice president, Kamala Harris, was nationally televised, further underscoring racial tensions in the U.S. and the need for DEI and unbleaching. As we noted, in 2021 the U.S. Justice Department closed the investigation into the murder of Emmett Till, an African American boy who was lynched for supposedly looking at a White woman (Jarrett, 2021). These and other social injustices, such as the cases of Trayvon Martin, Jonathan Ferrell, and others, point to the severity of the United States' racial and ethnic relations problems. As such, there remains a need for greater DEI work and unbleaching in education and beyond.

Throughout this book, we have provided examples of falsifications, omissions, and suppressed contributions (PtahHotep, Imhotep, Ahmes, the Olmec, etc.) and their role in human history, as well as in curricular design. As such, here are some final thoughts to consider to help illustrate why unbleaching is necessary. Former UNESCO general director Amadou-Mahtar M'bow (1992) notes that "for a long time all kinds of myths and prejudices concealed the true history of Africa from the world at large. African societies were looked upon as societies that could have no history" (p. xxiii). What is perhaps most unrecognized in African history is the fact there are non-White contributions that have been whitewashed throughout history. Thus the unbleaching project involves systemic curricular and institutional change. Again, this is not a racial project; it is a human project that promotes inclusion. As such, this benefits all students.

In fact, a U.S. Department of Education (2016) report indicates that students experience less discrimination and bias and have better overall learning outcomes when they perceive schools as having a strong commitment to diversity. As such, it is crucial for school leaders, policy makers, and teachers to work toward DEI and unbleaching educational practices. Aside from the teacher workforce and classroom pedagogy, the curriculum is also in need of unbleaching. This is evidenced by the prevalence of European history, which is often featured at the expense of non-White perspectives. For example, instead of crediting Africa for its role as the dawn of humanity, history instead inaccurately starts with Europe. As such, African accomplishments are often replaced with Europeans in state and national standards. Christopher Columbus, Hippocrates, and Pythagoras are just some of the names that commonly appear in curriculum standards that students must learn (Common Core State Standards, 2021; NCSS, 2017, 2018); meanwhile, PtahHotep, Imhotep, and the Olmec are frequently omitted (Common Core State Standards, 2021; NCSS, 2017, 2018). As a result of this sort of systemic removal, Greek philosophers are inaccurately considered the standard-bearers of knowledge throughout world history. The argument here is not to remove the Greek thinkers, but that there should be greater inclusion and multicultural perspectives.

There seems to be an egregious overstep in failing to *first* acknowledge African influences in European literature, religion, and philosophy (Onyeweueni, 2005). A more appropriate positioning of Africa in the curriculum should begin with evidence from anthropology and archaeology that this continent is the birthplace of humanity (NSF, 2001; Shared DNA, 2005). As noted throughout numerous primary sources, some Greek scholars were students of Egyptian teachers (Aristotle, 350 B.C.E./1966; Herodotus, 440 B.C.E./2014; Plato, 348 B.C.E./1968). In relation to unbleaching the curriculum and giving proper attribution to primary sources, it is important for the curriculum to reposition Africa and its contributions to humanity.

Through the process of whitewashing history, much of Black and Brown contributions have been omitted, and the ways in which Africans have been portrayed have also been inaccurate. As such, students learn about history through the lens of a White ethos, much of which minimizes Black and Brown people's voices. For example, Georg Wilhelm Friedrich Hegel (1892), who is known as a founding father of Western philosophy and idealism, notes in his *Lectures on the History of Philosophy* that Africa is an "unhistorical, undeveloped Spirit." Hegel also denigrates the contributions of Blacks to mainstream society. Such is the case with national and state curriculum standards that often marginalize African and Black contributions. This sort of misinformation is as troubling as it is damaging. While the role of Egypt, also called Kemet, meaning "Land of the Blacks" (Herodotus, 440 B.C.E./2014), in antiquity is well established (NSF, 2001), the curriculum hardly mentions the contributions of PtahHotep and Imhotep in history. To that end, unbleaching the curriculum attempts to recenter historical facts to start with a more accurate starting point.

To offer some closing thoughts, an excerpt from Plato's *Laws*, which most secondary and postsecondary students are programmatically exposed to, provides an excellent summation regarding the need for unbleaching. Plato presents an interesting dialogue between two Greek citizens, an Athenian and Clinias, in 348 B.C.E. The two discuss Egypt's high-quality education system comparatively with the Greeks. In the *Laws*, Plato explains:

> ATHENIAN. One ought to declare, then, that the freeborn children should learn as much of these subjects as the innumerable crowd of children in Egypt learn along with their letters. First, as regards counting, lessons have been invented for the merest infants to learn, by way of play and fun—modes of dividing up apples and chaplets, so that the same totals are adjusted to larger and smaller groups, and modes of sorting out boxers and wrestlers, in byes and pairs, taking them alternately or consecutively, in their natural order. Moreover, by way of play, the teachers mix together bowls made of gold, bronze, silver and the like, and others distribute them, as I said, by groups of a single kind, adapting the rules of elementary arithmetic to play; and thus they are of service to the pupils for their future tasks of drilling, leading and marching armies, or of household management, and they render them both more helpful in every way to themselves and more alert. The next step of the teachers is to clear away, by lessons in weights and measures, a certain kind of ignorance, both absurd and disgraceful, which is naturally inherent in all men touching lines, surfaces and solids.
>
> CLINIAS. What ignorance do you mean, and of what kind is it?
>
> ATHENIAN. My dear Clinias, when I was told quite lately of our condition in regard to this matter, I was utterly astounded myself: it seemed to me to be the condition of guzzling swine rather than of human beings, and I was ashamed, not only of myself, but of all the Greek world. (348 B.C.E./1968, p. 819)

As illustrated in the above conversation between the Athenian and Clinias, the Egyptians impressed travelers and people from other regions. The Hellenic world, as described by the Athenian, was too late in matters of educational reform, even before the first century. The Egyptians mastered effective ways to educate their students and made sure to embed *rigor* and *relevance* within the curriculum as early as infancy. Yet U.S. curriculum standards continuously cite the Greeks, with little to no attribution regarding the contributions of Egypt or the rest of Africa. Thus the process of unbleaching helps to correct the curriculum and whitewashed history and social studies content, which is helpful for all—students and teachers alike.

CHAPTER SUMMARY

In this final chapter of *Unbleaching the Curriculum: Enhancing Diversity, Equity, Inclusion, and Beyond in Schools and Society*, we addressed the importance of education reform in the context of unbleaching. Additionally, we presented unbleaching as a framework for promoting DEI in school processes and practices, to mitigate the effects of a hegemonic curriculum. In the context of unbleaching, federal education reform in curriculum design and teacher pedagogy can improve outcomes for all students. In sum, this chapter discussed how unbleaching can address contemporary issues in education reform, curriculum design, and teacher pedagogy. We hope that the contributions made in this book will help to make schools and society more humane and inclusive for all.

References

Acosta, M. M., Foster, M., & Houchen, D. F. (2018). "Why seek the living among the dead?" African American pedagogical excellence: Exemplar practice for teacher education. *Journal of Teacher Education, 69*(4), 341–353. https://doi.org/10.1177/0022487118761881

Adamo, D. T. (2001). *Africa and the Africans in the Old Testament*. Wipf and Stock Publishers.

Adichie, C. N. (2009). TEDTalks: Chimamanda Adichie—The danger of a single story [Video]. https://www.ted.com/talks/chimamanda_ngozi_adichie_the_danger_of_a_single_story?language=en#t-242721

Akbar, N. I. (1998). *Know thyself*. Mind Productions and Associates.

Akom, A. A. (2009). Critical hip hop pedagogy as a form of liberatory praxis. *Equity & Excellence in Education, 42*(1), 52–66. https://doi.org/10.1080/10665680802612519

Akua, C. (2020). Standards of Afrocentric education for school leaders and teachers. *Journal of Black Studies, 51*(2), 107–127. https://doi.org/10.1177/0021934719893572

Aldridge, S. (2014). *Trailblazers in medicine*. Rosen Publishing Group.

Alexander, M. (2012). *The new Jim Crow: Mass incarceration in the age of colorblindness*. The New Press.

Allen, C. D., & Eisenhart, M. (2017). Fighting for desired versions of a future self: How young women negotiated STEM-related identities in the discursive landscape of educational opportunity. *Mind, Culture, and Activity, 26*(3), 407–436. https://doi.org/10.1080/10508406.2017.1294985

Anderson, D. S. (2016). Black Olmecs and White Egyptians: A parable for professional archaeological responses to pseudoarchaeology. In J. J. Card & D. S. Anderson (Eds.), *Lost City, Found Pyramid: Understanding Alternative Archaeologies and Pseudoscientific Practices* (pp. 68–80). University of Alabama Press.

Anderson, J. D. (1988). *The education of Blacks in the South, 1860–1935*. University of North Carolina Press.

Apple, M. W. (2004). *Ideology and curriculum*. Routledge & Kegan Publishers.

Areddy, J. T. (2020, May 26). China rules out animal market and lab as coronavirus origin. *The Wall Street Journal*. https://www.wsj.com/articles/china rules-out-animal-market-and-lab-as-coronavirus-origin-11590517508

Aristotle. (1966). *Metaphysics* (Vol. 1, W. D. Ross, Trans.). Oxford Clarendon Press. (Original work published circa 350 B.C.E.).

Artiles, A. J. & Trent, S. (1994). Overrepresentation of minority students in special education: A continuing debate. *Journal of Special Education, 27*(4), 410–437.

Asante, M. K. (1990). *Kemet, Afrocentricity, and knowledge*. Africa World Press.

Asante, M. K. (1991). The Afrocentric idea in education. *The Journal of Negro Education, 60*(2), 170–180. https://doi.org/10.2307/2295608

Asante, M. K. (2000). *The Egyptian philosophers: Ancient African voices from Imhotep to Akhenaten*. African American Images.

Asante, M. K. (2017). *Revolutionary pedagogy: Primer for teachers of Black children*. Universal Write Publications.

Ash, A., & Wiggan, G. (2018). Race, multiculturalisms and the role of science in teaching diversity: Towards a critical postmodern science pedagogy. *Multicultural Education Review, 10*(2), 94–120. https://doi.org/10.1080/2005615X.2018.1460894

Ash, A., & Wiggan, G. (2021). Melanin and the malignity of social constructions of race. *Black History Bulletin, 84*(2), 5–8. https://doi.org/10.1353/bhb.2021.0001

Ash, A. A., II, Wiggan, G. A., & Watson-Vandiver, M. J. (2020). *Teacher education to enhance diversity in STEM: Applying a critical postmodern science pedagogy*. Routledge.

Asheri, D., Lloyd, A., & Corcella, A. (2007). *A commentary on Herodotus books I–IV* (Vol. 1). Oxford University Press.

Banks, J. A. (1993a). Multicultural education: Historical development, dimensions, and practice. *Review of Research in Education, 19*, 3–49. https://doi.org/10.2307/1167339

Banks, J. A. (1993b). The canon debate, knowledge construction, and multicultural education. *Educational Researcher, 22*(5), 4–14. https://doi.org/10.3102/0013189X022005004

Banks, J. A. (2010). Approaches to multicultural curriculum reform. In J. A. Banks & C. A. M. Banks (Eds.), *Multicultural education: Issues and perspectives* (7th ed., pp. 233–258). Wiley.

Banks, J. A., & Banks, C. A. M. (2010). *Multicultural education: Issues and perspectives* (7th ed.). Wiley.

Baptiste, S. A. (2010). *Moving beyond Black History month: How three teachers interpreted and implemented the New Jersey Amistad legislation*. Rutgers, The State University of New Jersey–New Brunswick.

Barton, P. A. (2001). *A history of the African-Olmecs: Black civilization of America from prehistoric times to the present era*. AuthorHouse.

Bell, D. (1980). *Brown v. Board of Education* and the interest-convergence dilemma. *Harvard Law Review, 93*(3), 518–534. https://doi.org/10.2307/1340546

Bell, D. (1995). Who's afraid of critical race theory? *University of Illinois Law Review, 1995*(4), 893–910.

Bell, D. (2004). *Silent covenants: Brown v. Board of Education and the unfulfilled hopes for racial reform*. Oxford University Press.

Bell, D. (2008). *And we are not saved: The elusive quest for racial justice*. Basic Books.

Bell, G. C. (2017). *Talking Black and White: An intercultural exploration of twenty-first-century racism, prejudice, and perception*. Rowman & Littlefield.

Bernasconi, R. (2020). Who invented the concept of race? In L. Back & J. Solomos (Eds.), *Theories of race and racism* (pp. 83–103). Routledge; Taylor and Francis Inc.

Blakemore, E. (2019, December 14). Who were the Moors? *National Geographic*. https://www.nationalgeographic.com/history/article/who-were-moors

Blatch, S. (2013). Great achievements in science and technology in ancient Africa. *ASBMB Today*. https://www.asbmb.org/asbmb-today/science/020113/great-achievements-in-stem-in-ancient-africa

Boser, U. (2011). Teacher diversity matters: A state-by-state analysis of teachers of color. *Center for American Progress*.

Brandt-Rauf, P. W., & Brandt-Rauf, S. I. (1987). History of occupational medicine: Relevance of Imhotep and the Edwin Smith Papyrus. *British Journal of Industrial Medicine, 44*(1), 68–70. https://doi.org/10.1136/oem.44.1.6

Braxton, P. N. (1990). Othello: The Moor and the metaphor. *South Atlantic Review, 55*(4), 1–17. https://doi.org/10.2307/3200442

Breasted, J. H. (1930). *The Edwin Smith Surgical Papyrus* (Facsimile and hieroglyphic transliteration with translation and commentary, in two volumes). The University of Chicago Press.

British Medical Journal. (1927). Imhotep: The physician-architect. *The British Medical Journal, 1*(3458), 734. https://doi.org/10.1136/bmj.1.3458.731

British Museum. (n.d.). Object: The Rhind Mathematical Papyrus. Museum number EA10057. https://www.britishmuseum.org/collection/object/Y_EA10057

Broderick, B. (2014). The African-American history requirement for students in the School District of Philadelphia: Is it worth the controversy? 2014 National Conference on Undergraduate Research.

Budge, E. A. W. (Ed.). (1855). *The chapters of* Coming Forth by Day: *Or the Theban recension of the* Book of the Dead (Vol. 28). K. Paul, Trench, Trübner & Company.

Budge, E. A. W. (1920). *By Nile and Tigris: A narrative of journeys in Egypt and Mesopotamia on behalf of the British Museum between the years 1886 and 1913* (Vol. 1). AMS Press Inc.

Budge, E. A. W. (1967). *The book of the dead: The papyrus of Ani in the British museum*. Courier Corporation.

Budge, E. A. W. (2015). *A history of Ethiopia: Nubia and Abyssinia* (Vol. 1). Routledge. (Original work published 1928)

Burns, D., Darling-Hammond, L., & Scott, C. (2019). Closing the opportunity gap: How positive outlier districts in California are pursuing equitable access to deeper learning [Research brief]. Learning Policy Institute.

Bush, G. W. (2001). *No Child Left Behind*. U.S. Department of Education, Office of the Secretary.

Byford, J., & Russell, W. (2007). The new social studies: A historical examination of curriculum reform. *Social Studies Research and Practice, 2*(1), 38–48. https://doi.org/10.1108/SSRP-01-2007-B0003

Carruthers, J. H. (1995). *Mdw Ntr, divine speech a historiographical reflection of African deep thought from the time of the pharaohs to the present.* Karnak House Publishers.

Cavalli-Sforza, L. L. (1998, September 29). The Chinese human genome diversity project. *Proceedings of the National Academy of Sciences, USA, 95*(20), 11501–11503. https://doi.org/10.1073/pnas.95.20.11501

Centers for Disease Control and Prevention. (2020a). Coronavirus (COVID-19). Centers for Disease Control and Prevention. https://www.cdc.gov/coronavirus/2019-ncov

Centers for Disease Control and Prevention. (2020b). Cases in the U.S. Centers for Disease Control and Prevention. https://www.cdc.gov/coronavirus/2019-ncov/cases-updates/cases-in-us.html

Chace, A. B., Bull, L., Manning, H. P., & Archibald, R. C. (1929). *The Rhind Mathematical Papyrus, British Museum 10057 and 10058; photographic facsimile, hieroglyphic transcription, transliteration, literal translation, free translation, mathematical commentary, and bibliography* [Print]. Mathematical Association of America.

Chang'ach, J. K. (2014). Contributions of Herodotus to African history. *Global Journal of Human-Social Science D: History, Archeology and Anthropology, 14*(5), 59–64.

Chang'ach, J. K. (2015). If ancient Egyptians were Negroes, then European civilization is but a derivation of African achievements. *Arts and Social Science Journal, 6*(2), 1–8. https://doi.org/10.4172/2151-6200.100098

Chapman, T. K. (2008). Desegregation and multicultural education: Teachers embracing and manipulating reforms. *The Urban Review, 40*(1), 42–63. https://doi.org/10.1007/s11256-007-0076-4

Chatterji, B. R. (1939, January). Jayavarman VII (1181–1201 AD) (The last of the great monarchs of Cambodia). In *Proceedings of the Indian History Congress* (Vol. 3, pp. 377–385). Indian History Congress.

Chebrolu, E. (2020). The racial lens of Dylann Roof: Racial anxiety and white nationalist rhetoric on new media. *Review of Communication, 20*(1), 47–68. https://doi.org/10.1080/15358593.2019.1708441

Chenoweth, K., & Theokas, C. (2013). How high-poverty schools are getting it done. *Educational Leadership, 70*(7), 56–59.

Children's Defense Fund. (2022). A message from Marian Wright Edelman. https://www.childrensdefense.org/staff/marian-wright-edelman

Chinweizu, I. (1987). *Decolonising the African mind.* Pero Press.

Clabough, J., Turner, T. N., Russell, W. B., III, & Waters, S. (Eds.). (2015). *Unpuzzling history with primary sources.* Information Age Publishing.

Clark, K., & Clark, M. (1950). Emotional factors in racial identity and preference in Negro children. *The Journal of Negro History, 19*(3), 341–350. https://doi.org/10.2307/2966491

Clarke, J. H. (1977). The University of Sankore at Timbuctoo: A neglected achievement in Black intellectual history. *The Western Journal of Black Studies, 1*(2), 142–146. http://search.proquest.com/docview/1311803723

Clarke, J. H. (1979). African-American historians and the reclaiming of African history. *Présence Africaine, 110*(2), 29–48. https://doi.org/10.3917/presa.110.0029

Clarke, J. H. (1991). *Notes for an African world revolution: Africans at the crossroads.* Africa World Press.

Clarke, J. H. (1995). *Christopher Columbus & the Afrikan Holocaust: Slavery & the rise of European capitalism.* A & B Distributors.

Coe, M. D., Urcid, J., & Koontz, R. (2019). *Mexico: From the Olmecs to the Aztecs.* Thames & Hudson.

Columbus, C. (1847). *Christopher Columbus: Four voyages to the New World: Letters and selected documents.* Peter Smith.

Common Core State Standards. (2021). Common core state standards initiative. https://learning.ccsso.org/common-core-state-standards-initiative

Cooper, J. (2014). Lost kingdoms of Central America. BBC. https://www.bbc.co.uk/programmes/b04hsz2v

Crenshaw, K. W. (2001). The first decade: Critical reflections, or a foot in the closing door. *University of California Los Angeles Law Review, 49*, 1343.

Crenshaw, K. (2016). The urgency of intersectionality. TEDWomen 2016. https://www.ted.com/talks/kimberle_crenshaw_the_urgency_of_intersectionality

Crenshaw, K., Gotanda, N., Peller, G., & Thomas, K. (Eds.). (1995). *Critical race theory: The key writings that formed the movement.* The New Press.

Creswell, J. W., & Poth, C. N. (2018). *Qualitative inquiry and research design: Choosing among five approaches.* Sage Publications.

Crocco, M., & Costigan, A. (2007). The narrowing of curriculum and pedagogy in the age of accountability urban educators speak out. *Urban Education, 42*(6), 512–535. https://doi.org/10.1177/0042085907304964

Crouch, E. (2014, August 20). Edwardsville teachers told to avoid discussing Ferguson events with students. *St. Louis Post.* http://www.stltoday.com/news/local/education/edwardsville-teachers-told-to-avoid-discussing-ferguson-events-with-students/article_1358925d-3e54-5823-9ce3-2f9938fc4c22.html

Danesi, M. (2018). *Ahmes' legacy: Puzzles and the mathematical mind.* Springer. https://doi.org/10.1007/978-3-319-93254-5

Darling-Hammond, L. (2007). Third annual Brown lecture in education research—The flat earth and education: How America's commitment to equity will determine our future. *Educational Researcher, 36*(6), 318–334.

Darling-Hammond, L. (2022, October 1). Breaking the legacy of teacher shortages. Association for Supervision and Curriculum Development. https://www.ascd.org/el/articles/breaking-the-legacy-of-teacher-shortages

Darling-Hammond, L., Burns, D., Campbell, C., Goodwin, A. L., Hammerness, K., Low, E.-L., McIntyre, A., Sato, M., & Zeichner, K. (2017). *Empowered educators: How high-performing systems shape teaching quality around the world.* John Wiley & Sons.

Davey D. (1991). The lost interview with Tupac Shakur. Hip Hop and Politics. www.hiphopandpolitics.wordpress.com

Davies, D. (1974). *The last of the Tasmanians*. Barnes & Noble Books, 1974.

Davis, A. (2000). Masked racism: Reflections on the prison industrial complex. [Article reprinted from Colorlines]. *Indigenous Law Bulletin 4*(27), 4–7.

Davis, F. J. (2010). *Who is black? One nation's definition*. Penn State Press.

Dee, T. S., Jacob, B., & Schwartz, N. L. (2013). The effects of NCLB on school resources and practices. *Educational Evaluation and Policy Analysis, 35*(2), 252–279. https://doi.org/10.3102/0162373712467080

de Freitas, E. L., Franco, A., & Teasdell, A. (2021). Black mental health matters: Bridging the mental health gap in the Black community. *Black History Bulletin, 84*(2), 18–21. https://doi.org/10.1353/bhb.2021.0009

Dei, G. J. S. (1994). Afrocentricity: A cornerstone of pedagogy. *Anthropology & Education Quarterly, 25*(1), 3–28. https://doi.org/10.1525/aeq.1994.25.1.05x0961y

Dei, S. D. (1996). *Antiracism education: Theory and practice*. Fernwood Publishers.

Dei, S. D., & Lordan, M. (Eds.). (2016). *Anti-colonial theory and decolonial praxis*. Peter Lang.

de la Croix, D., & Stelter, R. (2021). Scholars and Literati at the University of Göttingen (1734–1800). *Repertorium eruditorum totius Europae, 4*, 1–8. https://doi.org/10.14428/rete.v4i0/Gottingen

de Las Casas, B. (1992). *A brief account of the destruction of the Indies*. Penguin. (Original work published 1689)

Delgado, R., & Stefancic, J. (2017). *Critical race theory: An introduction*. New York University Press.

Delpit, L. (1988). The silenced dialogue: Power and pedagogy in educating other people's children. *Harvard Educational Review, 58*(3), 280–299. https://doi.org/10.17763/haer.58.3.c43481778r528qw4

Delpit, L. (2006). *Other people's children: Cultural conflict in the classroom*. The New Press.

Delpit, L. (Ed.). (2019). *Teaching when the world is on fire*. The New Press.

deMarrais, K., & LeCompte, M. (1999). *The way schools work: A sociological analysis of education* (3rd ed.). Longman.

Diehl, R. A. (2001). Were the Olmecs African? In B. Fagan (Ed.), *The seventy great mysteries of the ancient world: Unlocking the secrets of past civilizations* (pp. 171–172). Thames & Hudson.

Diehl, R. A. (2004). *The Olmecs: America's first civilization*. Thames & Hudson.

Diodorus, S. (1790). *Library of History, Volume I: Books 1–2.34* (C. H. Oldfather, Trans.). Loeb Classical Library 279. Harvard University Press. (Original work published circa 60/59 B.C.E.)

Diodorus, S. (1868). *Bibliotheca historica* (Vol. 5). Teubner. (Original work published circa 60/59 B.C.E.)

Diop, C. A. (1967). *Anteriority of Negro civilizations*. Presence Africaine.

Diop, C. A. (1974). *The African origin of civilization myth or reality*. Lawrence Hill Books.

Diop, C. A. (1981a). *Civilization or barbarism: An authentic anthropology*. Lawrence Hill Books.

Diop, C. A. (1981b). Origin of the Ancient Egyptians. In G. Mokhtar (Ed.), *General history of Africa: Vol. 2. Ancient civilizations of Africa, general history of Africa*. Heinemann.

Diop, C. A. (1989). *The cultural unity of Black Africa: The domains of patriarchy and of matriarchy in classical antiquity*. Karnak House.

Donnelly, R., & Patrinos, H. A. (2021). Learning loss during COVID-19: An early systematic review. *Prospects, 51*, 601–609. https://doi.org/10.21203/rs.3.rs-518655/v1

Donnor, J. K., & Dixson, A. (Eds.). (2013). *The resegregation of schools: Education and race in the twenty-first century*. Routledge.

Dorn, E., Hancock, B., Sarakatsannis, J., & Viruleg, E. (2020, December 8). COVID-19 and learning loss—Disparities grow and students need help. McKinsey & Company.

Dover, A. G., Henning, N., & Agarwal-Rangnath, R. (2016). Reclaiming agency: Justice-oriented social studies teachers respond to changing curricular standards. *Teaching and Teacher Education, 59*, 457–467. https://doi.org/10.1016/j.tate.2016.07.016

Drake, S. C. (1987). *Black folk here and there: An essay in history and anthropology* (Vol. 1). Center for Afro-American Studies, University of California, 1990.

Dreeben, R. (2002). *On what is learned in school*. Percheron Press. (Original work published 1968).

Du Bois, W. E. B. (1903). *The souls of black folk*. Oxford University Press.

Durden, T. (2008). Do your homework! Investigating the role of culturally relevant pedagogy in comprehensive school reform models serving diverse student populations. *The Urban Review, 40*(4), 403–419. https://doi.org/10.1007/s11256-008-0086-x

Dynamic Learning Maps Science Consortium (2019). *Dynamic learning maps essential elements for science*. University of Kansas.

Dyson, M. E. (2006). *Holler if you hear me: Searching for Tupac Shakur*. Civitas Books.

Education Week. (2021, September 26). Map: Where critical race theory is under attack. https://www.edweek.org/policy-politics/map-where-critical-race-theory-is-under-attack/2021/06

Edzard, S. (1997). *Gudea and his dynasty*. University of Toronto Press.

Egyptian Museum (n.d.). Karnak: The city of Temples. https://egyptianmuseum.org/explore/middle-kingdom-monuments-karnak

Elliott, D. (2020, June 17). 5 years after Charleston church massacre, what have we learned? NPR. https://www.npr.org/2020/06/17/878828088/5-years-after-charleston-church-massacre-what-have-we-learned

Ellis, T. (1989). The new black aesthetic. *Callaloo, 38*, 233–243. https://doi.org/10.2307/2931157

Evans, K. W. (1969). The racial factor in Othello. *Shakespeare Studies, 5*, 124–140.

Evans, R. (2017). *Exploration of African presence in Mesoamerica: The Olmecs*. Texas Institute for the Perseveration of History and Culture at Prairie View A&M University. https://www.pvamu.edu/tiphc/research-projects/afro-mexicans-afromestizos/exploration-of-african-presence-in-meso-america-the-olmecs

Fanon, F. (2007). *The wretched of the earth*. Grove/Atlantic.

Feldman, R. P., & Goodrich, J. T. (1999). The Edwin Smith surgical papyrus. *Child's Nervous System, 15*(6–7), 281–284. https://doi.org/10.1007/s003810050395

Figlio, D. (2017). The importance of a diverse teaching force. Brookings Institute. https://www.brookings.edu/research/the-importance-of-a-diverse-teaching-force

Flick, U. (2002). *An introduction to qualitative research* (2nd ed.). Sage Publications.

Freire, P. (2018). *Pedagogy of the oppressed*. Bloomsbury Publishing USA. (Original work published 1970)

Fry, R., Kennedy, B., & Funk, C. (2021). STEM jobs see uneven progress in increasing gender, racial and ethnic diversity. Pew Research Center. https://www.pewresearch.org/science/2021/04/01/stem-jobs-see-uneven-progress-in-increasing-gender-racial-and-ethnic-diversity

Gaillard, F. (2006). *The dream long deferred: The landmark struggle for desegregation in Charlotte, North Carolina*. University of South Carolina Press.

García, E., & Weiss, E. (2020). *COVID-19 and student performance, equity, and US education policy: Lessons from pre-pandemic research to inform relief, recovery, and rebuilding*. Economic Policy Institute.

Garrett, R. B. (1978). Imhotep—Father of medicine. *Negro History Bulletin, 41*(5), 876.

Garza, A. (2014). A herstory of the #BlackLivesMatter movement. https://collectiveliberation.org/wp-content/uploads/2015/01/Garza_Herstory_of_the_BlackLivesMatter_Movement.pdf

Gay, G. (2018). *Culturally responsive teaching* (2nd ed.). Teachers College Press.

Gershenson, S., Hart, C. M. D., Hyman, J., Lindsay, C., & Papageorge, N. W. (2021). The long-run impacts of same-race teachers (Working Paper 25254). National Bureau of Economic Research. http://www.nber.org/papers/w25254

Gillings, R. J. (1972). *Mathematics in the time of the pharaohs*. MIT Press.

Gomez, M. A. (2019). *Reversing sail: A history of the African Diaspora* (Vol. 14). Cambridge University Press.

Gonzalez Lauk, R. (1988). Proyecto arqueologico La Venta. In A. G. Mastache (Ed.), *Arqueologia* (Vol. 4, pp. 121–165). INAH, Mexico City.

Gramsci, A. (1971). *Selections from the prison notebooks of Antonio Gramsci* (O. Hoare & G. Nowell Smith, Trans.). Lawrence & Wishart.

Graness, A. (2016). Writing the history of philosophy in Africa: Where to begin? *Journal of African Cultural Studies, 28*(2), 132–146. https://doi.org/10.1080/13696815.2015.1053799

Grant, C. A. (2015). *Multiculturalism in education and teaching: The selected works of Carl A. Grant*. Routledge.

Greppo, J. H. (1830). *Essay on the hieroglyphic system of M. Champollion, Jun: And on the advantages which it offers to sacred criticism*. Perkins & Marvin.

Grimes, K. (2014). "But do the Lord care?" Tupac Shakur as theologian of the crucified people. *Political Theology, 15*(4), 326–352. https://doi.org/10.1179/1462317X14Z.00000000082

Grisby, C. (2020). State board approves African American studies high school course despite controversy. *Spectrum News 1*. https://spectrumlocalnews.com/tx/san-antonio/news/2020/04/29/state-board-approves-african-american-studies-high-school-course-despite-controversy-

Grove, D. (2014). *Discovering the Olmecs: An unconventional history* (1st ed.). University of Texas Press.

Gurin, P., Dey, E. L., Hurtado, S., & Gurin, G. (2002). Diversity and higher education: Theory and impact on educational outcomes. *Harvard Educational Review, 72*(3), 330–366. https://doi.org/10.17763/haer.72.3.01151786u134n051

Guthrie, R. V. (2004). *Even the rat was white: A historical view of psychology*. Pearson Education.

Guy, J. (2010). *Afeni Shakur: Evolution of a revolutionary*. Simon & Schuster.

Hamilton, V. (1993). May Hill Arbuthnot honor lecture: Everything of value: Moral realism in the literature for children. *Journal of Your Services in Libraries, 6*, 363–377.

Hannah-Jones, N. (2021). *The 1619 project: A new origin story*. One World.

Hansen, M., Levesque, E., Valant, J., & Quintero, D. (2018). *The 2018 Brown Center report on American education: How well are American students learning?* The Brookings Institution.

Harper, R. F. (Ed.). (1999). *The Code of Hammurabi, King of Babylon: About 2250 BC: Autographed text, transliteration, translation, glossary index of subjects, lists of proper names, signs, numuerals . . .* The Lawbook Exchange, Ltd.

Hartocollis, A. (2022, August 31). The first A.P. African American Studies class is coming this fall. *New York Times*. https://www.nytimes.com/2022/08/31/us/ap-african-american-studies.html

Haslip-Viera, G., de Montellano, B. O., & Barbour, W. (1997). Robbing Native American cultures: Van Sertima's Afrocentricity and the Olmecs. *Current Anthropology, 38*(3), 419–441. https://doi.org/10.1086/204626

Hegel, G. W. F. (1892). *Hegel's lectures on the history of philosophy: Volume one.* (E.S. Haldane, Trans.). Routledge & Kegan Paul.

Henderson, J., Lynch, J., & Parks, B. (2020, July 9). An officer told George Floyd it took "a lot of oxygen to talk," body camera transcripts show. CNN. https://www.cnn.com/2020/07/08/us/george-floyd-policebody-camera-transcripts/index.html

Herczog, M. M. (2013a). The C3 framework for social studies state standards. *Social Education, 77*(6), 316.

Herczog, M. M. (2013b). The links between the C3 framework and the NCSS national curriculum standards for social studies. *Social Education, 77*(6), 331–333.

Herczog, M. M. (2013c). Q and A about the college, career and civic life (C3) framework for social studies state standards. *Social Education, 77*(4), 218–219.

Herodotus. (2014). *The histories of Herodotus*. Macmillan Company. (Original work published circa 440 B.C.E.)

Hertslet, E. (1909). *The map of Africa by treaty*. Routledge.

Hickman, C. B. (1996). The devil and the one drop rule: Racial categories, African Americans, and the US census. *Michigan Law Review, 95*, 1161. https://doi.org/10.2307/1290008

Hill, E., Tiefenthäler, A., Triebert, C., Jordan, D., Willis, H., & Stein, R. (2020, May 31). How George Floyd was killed in police custody. *New York Times*. https://www.nytimes.com/2020/07/08/us/george-floyd-bodycamera-transcripts.html

Hill, M. L. (2009). *Beats, rhymes, and classroom life: Hip-hop pedagogy and the politics of identity*. Teachers College Press.

Hilliard, A. G. (1989). Kemetic (Egyptian) historical revision: Implications for cross-cultural evaluation and research in education. *Evaluation Practice, 10*(2), 7–23. https://doi.org/10.1016/S0886-1633(89)80048-0

Hilliard, A. G., III. (2000). Excellence in education versus high-stakes standardized testing. *Journal of Teacher Education, 51*(4), 293–304. https://doi.org/10.1177/0022487100051004005

Hilliard, A. G., & Sizemore, B. (1984). *Saving the African American child*. National Alliance of Black School Educators, Task Force on Black Academic and Cultural Excellence.

Hilliard, A. G., Williams, L., & Damali, N. (1987). *The teachings of PtahHotep: The oldest book in the world*. Blackwood Press.

Hilliard, C. B. (Ed.). (1998). *Intellectual traditions of pre-colonial Africa*. McGraw-Hill Humanities, Social Sciences & World Languages.

hooks, b. (2014). *Teaching to transgress: Education as the practice of freedom*. Routledge.

Hotz, R. L. (1998, September 29). Chinese roots lie in Africa, research says. *Los Angeles Times*. https://www.latimes.com/archives/la-xpm-1998-sep-29-mn-27603-story.html

Howell, C., Johanson, D., & Wong, K. (2018). Hadar: The legacy of human ancestors (4,000,000–100,000 BCE). In A. MacKinnon & E. Mcclarnand Mackinnon (Eds.), *Places of Encounter* (pp. 1–16). Routledge.

Hsieh, H. F., & Shannon, S. E. (2005). Three approaches to qualitative content analysis. *Qualitative Health Research, 15*(9), 1277–1288. https://doi.org/10.1177/1049732305276687

Huerta, A. (2020, May 15). The right to ethnic studies in higher education. *Inside Higher Ed*. https://www.insidehighered.com/advice/2020/05/15/why-students-should-be-required-take-ethnic-studies-opinion

Human Rights Watch (2020). Human Rights Watch world report 2020 events of 2019. Human Rights Watch. https://www.hrw.org/sites/default/files/world_report_download/hrw_world_report_2020_0.pdf

Hurry, J. B. (1926). *Imhotep: The vizier and physician of King Zoser and afterwards the Egyptian god of medicine*. Oxford University Press, H. Milford.

Hurtado, S., Newman, C. B., Tran, M. C., & Chang, M. J. (2010). Improving the rate of success for underrepresented racial minorities in STEM fields: Insights from a national project. *New Directions for Institutional Research, 2010*(148), 5–15. https://doi.org/10.1002/ir.357

Ibekwe, C. (2018). Examining the Charleston AME tragedy victims' forgiveness of Dylann Roof. In B. D. Lundy, A. G. Adebayo, & S. W. Hayes (Eds.), *Atone: Religion, conflict, and reconciliation* (pp. 153–172). Lexington Books.

Ighodaro, E., & Wiggan, G. (2011). *Curriculum violence: America's new civil rights issue*. Nova Science Publishers.

Imhotep image. https://commons.wikimedia.org/wiki/File:Imhotep.JPG

Ingold, J. (2018). Hacking the middle school social studies code. C3 Teachers. http://www.c3teachers.org/hacking-the-middle-school-social-studies-code

Inomata, T., Triadan, D., Aoyama, K., Castillo, V., & Yonenobu, H. (2013). Early ceremonial constructions at Ceibal, Guatemala, and the origins of lowland Maya Civilization. *Science, 340*(6131), 467–471. https://doi.org/10.1126/science.1234493

Israel, S. (2017, November 1). Building America's future: STEM education intervention is a win-win (Public policy initiative). University of Pennsylvania's Wharton School of Public Policy. https://publicpolicy.wharton.upenn.edu/live/news/2188-building-americas-future-stem-education

Jackson, J. G. (2017). *Ethiopia and the origin of civilization*. Martino Fine Books. (Original work published 1939)

Jackson, J. P., Weidman, N. M., & Rubin, G. (2005). The origins of scientific racism. *The Journal of Blacks in Higher Education, 50*(50), 66–79.

Jackson, T. O., & Boutte, G. S. (2009). Liberation literature: Positive cultural messages in children's and young adult literature at freedom schools. *Language Arts, 87*(2), 108–116. http://www.jstor.org/stable/41483549

Jarrett, L. (2021, December 7). Justice department closes investigation into Emmett Till killing after failing to prove key witness lied. CNN. https://www.cnn.com/2021/12/06/politics/emmett-till-case-closed/index.html

Jeong, A. (2021, August 5). Tennessee could withhold millions from schools found to violate guidelines on teaching critical race theory. *The Washington Post*. https://www.washingtonpost.com/nation/2021/08/05/tennessee-critical-race-theory

Johanson, D., & Wong, K. (2010). *Lucy's legacy: The quest for human origins*. Broadway Books.

Johnson, A. (2018, March 9). Oconomowoc schools impose limits on "privilege" discussions after parents complain. *Milwaukee Journal Sentinel*. https://www.jsonline.com/story/news/education/2018/03/09/oconomowoc-schools-impose-limits-privilege-discussions-after-parents-complain/407222002

Johnson, C. R. (2009). The first Africans: African Archaeology from the earliest toolmakers to most recent foragers. *African Studies Review, 52*(2), 189–190. https://doi.org/10.1353/arw.0.0190

Johnston, B. J. (2002). Absent from school: Educational policy and comprehensive reform. *The Urban Review, 34*(3), 205–230. https://doi.org/10.1023/A:1020651106756

Jones, E. D. (1965). *Othello's countrymen: The African in English Renaissance drama*. Oxford University Press.

Jones, E. D. (1971). *The Elizabethan image of Africa*. University of Virginia Press.

Jones, J. (2021, December 15). Sen. Raphael Warnock takes Manchin, Sinema to task over immoral conservatism. MSNBC. https://www.msnbc.com/the-reidout/reidout-blog/raphael-warnock-manchin-sinema-speech-rcna8711

Joyce, R. A., & Henderson, J. S. (2010). Being "Olmec" in early formative period Honduras. *Ancient Mesoamerica, 21*(1), 187–200. http://dx.doi.org.librarylink.uncc.edu/10.1017/S0956536110000052

Kamugisha, A. K. (2001). The early peoples of Pre-Columbian America: Ivan Van Sertima and his critics. *The Journal of Caribbean History, 35*(2), 234.

Kendi, I. X. (2017). *Stamped from the beginning: The definitive history of racist ideas in America*. Random House.

Kendi, I. X. (2019). *How to be an antiracist*. One World.

King, J. E. (1991). Dysconscious racism: Ideology, identity, and the miseducation of teachers. *The Journal of Negro Education, 60*(2), 133–146. https://doi.org/10.2307/2295605

King, J. E. (2015). *Dysconscious racism, Afrocentric praxis, and education for human freedom: Through the years I keep on toiling: The selected works of Joyce E. King.* Routledge.

King, J. E., & Swartz, E. E. (2014). *"Re-membering" history in student and teacher learning: An Afrocentric culturally informed praxis*. Routledge.

King, J. E., & Swartz, E. E. (2015). *The Afrocentric praxis of teaching for freedom: Connecting culture to learning*. Routledge.

King, J. E., & Swartz, E. (2018). *Heritage knowledge in the curriculum: Retrieving an African episteme*. Routledge.

King, L. J. (2017). The status of black history in US schools and society. *Social Education, 81*(1), 14–18.

Kluger, R. (2011). *Simple justice: The history of Brown v. Board of Education and Black America's struggle for equality*. Vintage.

Kozol, J. (2005). *The shame of the nation: The restoration of apartheid schooling in America*. Crown.

Krippendorff, K. (2018). *Content analysis: An introduction to its methodology*. Sage.

Krogstad, J. M. (2019). Reflecting a demographic shift, 109 U.S. counties have become majority nonwhite since 2000. Pew Research Center. https://www.pewresearch.org/fact-tank/2019/08/21/u-s-counties-majority-nonwhite/

Kubal, T. (2008). *Cultural movements and collective memory: Christopher Columbus and the rewriting of the national origin myth*. Springer.

Kunjufu, J. (2020). *COVID 1619 curriculum: When racism began in America*. Independent Publishers Group.

Ladson-Billings, G. (1998). Just what is critical race theory and what's it doing in a nice field like education? *International Journal of Qualitative Studies in Education, 11*(1), 7–24. https://doi.org/10.1080/095183998236863

Ladson-Billings, G. (Ed.). (2003). *Critical race theory: Perspectives on social studies*. Information Age Publishing.

Ladson-Billings, G. (2009). *The dreamkeepers: Successful teachers of African American children*. Jossey-Bass Publishers.

Ladson-Billings, G. (2016). And then there is this thing called the curriculum: Organization, imagination, and mind. *Educational Researcher, 45*(2), 100–104. https://doi.org/10.3102/0013189X16639042

Ladson-Billings, G., & Tate, W. (1995). Toward a critical race theory of education. *The Teachers College Record, 97*(1), 47–68. https://doi.org/10.1177/016146819509700104

LaForce, M., Noble, E., King, H., Century, J., Blackwell, C., Holt, S., Ibrahim, A., & Loo, S. (2016). The eight essential elements of inclusive STEM high schools. *International Journal of STEM Education, 3*(21), 1–11. https://doi.org/10.1186/s40594-016-0054-z

Lane-Poole, S. (1893). *The Moors in Spain*. TF Unwin.

Lang, C. (2020, September 29). President Trump has attacked critical race theory. Here's what to know about the intellectual movement. *Time.* https://time.com/5891138/critical-race-theory-explained

Lateiner, D. (2016). *The historical method of Herodotus*. University of Toronto Press.

Leatherby, L., Ray, A., Singhvi, A., Triebert, C., Watkins, D., & Willis, H. (2021, January 12). How a presidential rally turned into a capitol rampage. *New York Times.* https://www.nytimes.com/interactive/2021/01/12/us/capitol-mob-timeline.html

Leavy, P. (2007). *Iconic events: Media, politics, and power in retelling history*. Lexington Books.

Lee, J., & Reeves, T. (2012). Revisiting the impact of NCLB high-stakes school accountability, capacity, and resources: State NAEP 1990–2009 reading and math achievement gaps and trends. *Educational Evaluation and Policy Analysis, 34*(2), 209–231. https://doi.org/10.3102/0162373711431604

Lemert, C. (2004). *Social theory: The multicultural and classic readings* (4th ed.). Westview Press.

Loewen, J. (2008). *Lies my teacher told me: Everything your American history textbook got wrong*. The New Press.

Long, E. R. (2017). *Visions of the possible: Case studies of how social studies teachers enact the C3 framework*. Proquest.

Lorde, A. (1984). *Sister outsider: Essays and speeches*. Crossing Press.

Love, B. L. (2019). *We want to do more than survive: Abolitionist teaching and the pursuit of educational freedom*. Beacon Press.

Lynn, M., & Dixon, A. (Eds.). (2013). *Handbook of critical race theory in education*. Routledge.

Magness, P., & Page, S. (2011). *Colonization after emancipation: Lincoln and the movement for black resettlement*. University of Missouri Press.

Manilius, M. (1977). *Astronomica*. Harvard University Press. (Original work published circa 40 C.E.)

Marshall, J. D., Sears, J. T., & Schubert, W. H. (2007). *Turning points in curriculum: A contemporary American memoir* (2nd ed.). Merrill/Prentice Hall.

Martinez, A. Y. (2014). Critical race theory: Its origins, history, and importance to the discourses and rhetorics of race. *Frame: Journal of Literary Studies, 27*(2), 9–27.

Matsuda, M. J. (1991). Voices of America: Accent, antidiscrimination law, and a jurisprudence for the last reconstruction. *Yale Law Journal, 100*(5), 1329–1407. https://doi.org/10.2307/796694

Mayring, P. (2014). *Qualitative content analysis: Theoretical foundation, basic procedures and software solution*. https://www.psychopen.eu/fileadmin/user_upload/books/mayring/ssoar-2014-mayring-Qualitative_content_analysis_theoretical_foundation.pdf.

M'Bantu, A. (2019). *The aboriginal Black Olmec civilization*. Pomegranate Publishing.

Mbiti, J. S. (2015). *Introduction to African religion*. Waveland Press.

M'bow, A. M. (1992). Preface. In B. A. Ogot (Ed.), *General history of Africa: Africa from the sixteenth to the eighteenth century* (pp. xxiii–xxix). Heinemann International Literature and Textbooks.

McComas, W. F. (2014). Pedagogical content knowledge (PCK). In W. F. McComas (Ed.), *The language of science education* (p. 71). Sense Publishers.

McGuinn, P. (2012). Stimulating reform: Race to the Top, competitive grants and the Obama education agenda. *Educational Policy, 26*(1), 136–159. https://doi.org/10.1177/0895904811425911

McGuinn, P. (2016). From No Child Left Behind to the Every Student Succeeds Act: Federalism and the education legacy of the Obama administration. *Publius: The Journal of Federalism, 46*(3), 392–415. https://doi.org/10.1093/publius/pjw014

McIntosh, P. (1988). White privilege: Unpacking the invisible knapsack. In *White privilege and male privilege: A personal account of coming to see correspondences through work in Women's Studies*. Wellesley College Center for Research on Women.

McIntosh, P. (2002). White privilege: Unpacking the invisible knapsack. In P. S. Rothenberg (Ed.), *White privilege: Essential readings on the other side of racism* (pp. 97–101). Worth Publishers

McKenna, T. (2015). Tupac Shakur: History's poet. In *Art, literature and culture from a Marxist perspective* (pp. 70–80). Palgrave Macmillan.

Melgar y Serrano, J. M. (1869a). Antiguedades Mexicanos. *Boletin de la Sociedad Mexicana de Geografia y Estadistica, 2*(1), 292–297.

Melgar y Serrano, J. M. (1869b). Primer reporte sobre un artefacto Olmeca. *Seminario Ilustrado, México*, 1869. https://arqueologiamexicana.mx/mexico-antiguo/jose-maria-melgar-y-serrano-viajero-coleccionista-o-saqueador

Melgar y Serrano, J. M. (1869c). Study on the antiquity and origin of the Ethiopian-type colossal head that exists in Hueyapam. *Boletin de la Sociedad Mexicana de Geografia y Estadistica, 2*(3), 104–109.

Melgar y Serrano, J. M. (1871). Estudio sobre la Antiguedad y el Origen de la Cabeza Colosal de Tipo Etiópioc que Existe en Hueyapan, del Cantón de los Tuxtla. *Boletin de la Sociedad Mexicana de Geografia y Estadistica, 2*(3), 104–109.

Meltzer, E. S., & Sanchez, G. M. (2014). *The Edwin Smith Papyrus: Updated translation of the trauma treatise and modern medical commentaries*. ISD LLC.

Meredith, M. (2011). *Born in Africa: The quest for the origins of human life*. Public Affairs.

Merriam, S., & Tisdell, E. (2016). *Qualitative research: A guide to design and implementation* (4th ed.). Jossey-Bass.

Mertens, D. M. (2014). *Research and evaluation in education and psychology: Integrating diversity with quantitative, qualitative, and mixed methods*. Sage Publications.

Milner, H. R., IV. (2012). But what is urban education? *Urban Education, 47*(3), 556–561. https://doi.org/10.1177/0042085912447516

Milner, H. R., IV. (2013). Scripted and narrowed curriculum reform in urban schools. *Urban Education, 48*(2), 163–170. https://doi.org/10.1177/0042085913478022

Mokhtar, G. (1981). *General history of Africa: Ancient civilizations of Africa*. UNESCO.

Monkman, K., & Stromquist, N. P. (Eds.). (2000). *Globalization and education: Integration and contestation across cultures*. Rowman & Littlefield.

Morris, I. (2013). *The measure of civilization*. Princeton University Press.

Morris, M. (2016). *Pushout: The criminalization of Black girls in schools*. The New Press.

Most, G. W. (1997). One hundred years of fractiousness: Disciplining polemics in nineteenth-century German classical scholarship. *Transactions of the American Philological Association (1974–2014), 127*, 349–361. https://doi.org/10.2307/284398

Murphy, M. P. (2020). COVID-19 and emergency eLearning: Consequences of the securitization of higher education for post-pandemic pedagogy. *Contemporary Security Policy, 41*(3), 492–505.

Muttoni, G., Scardia, G., & Kent, D. V. (2010). Human migration into Europe during the late Early Pleistocene climate transition. *Palaeogeography, Palaeoclimatology, Palaeoecology, 296*(1–2), 79–93.

Myer, I. (2010). *Oldest books in the world: An account of the religion, wisdom, philosophy, ethics, psychology, manners, proverbs, sayings, refinement, etc., of the Ancient Egyptians: as set forth and inscribed upon, some of the oldest existing monuments, papyri, and other records of that people . . . together with facsimiles and translations of some of the oldest books in the world. Also a study . . . of the Book of the Dead*. E. W. Dayton Publishers. (Original work published 1900)

Nascimento, E. L. (2007). *The sorcery of color: Identity, race, and gender in Brazil*. Temple University Press.

National Assessment of Educational Progress. (2022a). National Assessment of Educational Progress report card mathematics. https://www.nationsreportcard.gov/mathematics/nation/achievement/?grade=12

National Assessment of Educational Progress. (2022b). National Assessment of Educational Progress report card reading. https://www.nationsreportcard.gov/reading/nation/achievement/?grade=4

National Association for Multicultural Education. (2019). I teach science. Can I be a multicultural educator? The National Association for Multicultural Education: Advancing and Advocating for Social Justice and Equity. https://www.nameorg.org/learn/i_teach_science_can_i_be_a_mu.php

National Center for Education Statistics. (2018). The condition of education 2018: Science performance. U.S. Department of Education. https://nces.ed.gov/pubs2018/2018144.pdf

National Center for Education Statistics. (2020). Characteristics of public and private elementary and secondary school teachers in the United States: Results from the 2017–18 National Teacher and Principal Survey. https://nces.ed.gov/pubs2020/2020142.pdf

National Council for the Social Studies. (2017). *College, career and civic life (C3) framework for social studies state standards: Guidance for enhancing the rigor of K–12 civics, economics, geography and history*. National Council for the Social Studies. https://www.socialstudies.org/sites/default/files/2017/Jun/c3-framework-for-social-studies-rev0617.pdf

National Council for the Social Studies. (2018). *National curriculum standards for social studies: A framework for teaching, learning, and assessment*. National Council for the Social Studies.

National Human Genome Research Institute. (2006/2011). Whole genome association studies. http://www.genome.gov/17516714

National Museum of Anthropology of Mexico City. (2019). https://museu.ms/museum/details/16762/national-museum-of-anthropology

National Museum of Ethiopia at Addis Ababa. (2019). Replica of Olmec head donated to Ethiopia by Mexico.

National Research Council. (2012). *A framework for K–12 science education: practices, cross-cutting concepts, and core ideas*. National Research Council.

National Science Foundation. (2001, July 12). Earliest human ancestors discovered in Ethiopia: Discovery of bones and teeth date fossils back more than 5.2 million years. *Science Daily*. https:www.sciencedaily.com/releases/2001/07/010712080134.htm

National Science Foundation. (2020a). U.S. and global education: Degrees awarded. National Science Board. https://ncses.nsf.gov/pubs/nsb20201/u-s-and-global-education

National Science Foundation. (2020b). U.S. science and engineering workforce. National Science Board. https://ncses.nsf.gov/pubs/nsb20201/u-s-s-e-workforce

National Science Foundation. (2020c). *STEM education for the future: 2020 visioning report*. https://www.nsf.gov/ehr/Materials/STEM%20Education%20for%20the%20Future%20-%202020%20Visioning%20Report.pdf

National Science and Technology Council (US). (2018). Charting a course for success: America's strategy for STEM education. Executive Office of the President. https://www.whitehouse.gov/wp-content/uploads/2018/12/STEM-Education-Strategic-Plan-2018.pdf

Neel, M. A., & Palmeri, A. (2017). Meeting the demands of the C3 framework in elementary social studies methods. *Social Studies Research and Practice, 12*(3), 358–371. https://doi.org/10.1108/SSRP-08-2017-0047

Nei, M., & Livshits, G. (1989). Genetic relationships of Europeans, Asians and Africans and the origin of modern Homo sapiens. *Human Heredity, 39*(5), 276–281. https://doi.org/10.1159/000153872

Newman, J. R. (1952). The Rhind papyrus. *Scientific American, 187*(2), 24–27.

Neuburger, M. (1943). British medicine and the Göttingen medical school in the eighteenth century. *Bulletin of the History of Medicine, 14*(4), 449–466.

Neumann, J. W. (2013). Advocating for a more effective critical pedagogy by examining structural obstacles to critical educational reform. *The Urban Review, 45*(5), 728–740. https://doi.org/10.1007/s11256-013-0244-7

Newkirk, P. (2015). *Spectacle: The astonishing life of Ota Benga*. New York University.

New York Public Library Archives and Manuscripts. (2020). Twenty-first century foundation (New York, N.Y.) records: 1971–1992. http://archives.nypl.org/scm/20939

New York Times. (1981, March 8). Van Sertima wins prize for book on Africa; Van Sertima wins $7,500 book prize. https://www.nytimes.com/1981/03/08/books/van-sertima-wins-prize-for-book-on-africa-van-sertima-wins-7500-book-prize.html

Obenga, T., & Saakana, A. S. (1991). *Ancient Egypt and Black Africa: A student's handbook for the study of Ancient Egypt in philosophy, linguistics, and gender relations*. Karnak House.

Ohito, E. O. (2019). "I just love Black people!": Love, pleasure, and critical pedagogy in urban teacher education. *The Urban Review, 51*(4), 123–145. https://doi.org/10.1007/s11256-018-0492-7

Omi, M., & Winant, H. (2014). *Racial formation in the United States*. Routledge.

Onyeweuenyi, I. C. (2005). *The African origin of Greek philosophy: An exercise on afrocentrism*. University of Nigeria Press.

Oppel, R. A., Jr., & Barker, K. (2020, July 8). New transcripts detail last moments for George Floyd. *New York Times*. https://www.nytimes.com/2020/07/08/us/george-floyd-bodycamera-transcripts.html

Orfield, G., & Yun, J. T. (1999). *Resegregation in American schools*. The Civil Rights Project. Harvard University. https://escholarship.org/uc/item/6d01084d

Ortiz de Montellano, B. R., Haslip-Viera, G., and Barbour, W. (1997). They were *NOT* here before Columbus: Afrocentric hyperdiffusionism in the 1990s. *Ethnohistory, 44*(2), 199–234. https://doi.org/10.2307/483368

Osler, W. (1921). *The evolution of modern medicine*. Yale University Press. (Original work published 1913)

Paris, D., & Alim, H. S. (Eds.). (2017). *Culturally sustaining pedagogies: Teaching and learning for justice in a changing world*. Teachers College Press.

Park, P. K. (2013). *Africa, Asia, and the history of philosophy: Racism in the formation of the philosophical canon, 1780–1830*. SUNY Press.

Patton, L. D., Donor, J., Dixson, A., & Anderson, C. (2016). Disrupting postsecondary prose: Toward a critical race theory of higher education. *Urban Education, 51*(3), 315–342. https://doi.org/10.1177/0042085915602542

Peet, T. E. (1923). *The Rhind Mathematical Papyrus, British Museum 10057 and 10058; introduction, transcription, translation and commentary by T. Eric Peet*. The University Press of Liverpool; Hodder & Stoughton. https://doi.org/10.1177/0042085915602542

Peltier, L. F. (1990). *Fractures: A history and iconography of their treatment* (No. 1). Norman Publishing.

Perez, J., Jr., & Guadiano, N. (2020, September 17). Trump blasts 1619 Project as DeVos praises alternative Black history curriculum. *Politico*. https://www.politico.com/news/2020/09/17/devos-black-history-1776-unites-417186

Phelps, R. H. (1954). The idea of the modern university—Göttingen and America. *The Germanic Review: Literature, Culture, Theory, 29*(3), 175–190. https://doi.org/10.1080/19306962.1954.11786745

Pimienta-Bey, J. V. (1992). Moorish Spain: Academic source and foundation for the rise and success of western European universities in the middle ages. In I. Van Sertima (Ed.), *Golden age of the Moor* (pp. 182–247). Transaction Publishers.

Pimienta-Bey, J. V. (2002). *Othello's children in the" New World": Moorish history & identity in the African American experience*. AuthorHouse.

Pinch, G. (2002). *Handbook of Egyptian mythology*. ABC-CLIO Publishers.

Pitkin, R. (2021, August 28). 5 things to know: HB 324 passes NC Senate, would restrict lessons on race in school. https://qcnerve.com/weekly-news-roundup-hb-324

Plato. (1968). *Laws* (R. G. Bury, Trans.). Harvard University Press. (Original work published circa 348 B.C.E.)

Potter, P., & Smith, W. D. (1923). *Hippocrates* (Vol. 1). Heinemann.

Ptahhotep, Hilliard, A. G., Williams, L. O., & Damali, N. (1987). *The teachings of Ptahhotep: The oldest book in the world*. Blackwood Press.

Qiu, J. (2016, July 13). How China is rewriting the book on human origins. *Scientific American*. https://www.scientificamerican.com/article/how-china-is-rewriting-the-book-on-human-origins

Rashidi, R. (1985). Africans in early Asian civilizations: A historical overview. *Journal of African Civilizations, 7*(1), 15–52.

Rashidi, R. (2011). *Black star: The African presence in early Europe*. Books of Africa.

Rashidi, R. (2012). *African star over Asia: The black presence in the east*. Books of Africa.

Rashidi, R. (2016). Ivan Van Sertima and the Olmec world: A photo essay. *Africology: The Journal of Pan African Studies, 9*(4), 364–372. https://link.gale.com/apps/doc/A461364171/LitRC?u=char69915&sid=LitRC&xid=f6b1c2e4

Rawlinson, G. (2018). *The origin of nations*. Franklin Classics Trade Press.

Rawlinson, G., & Rawlinson, H. (1858). *History of Herodotus* (Vol. 1). John Murray.

Rawlinson, H. C., & Wilkinson, J. G. (1861). *The history of Herodotus* (Vol. 1).

Reardon, S. F., Grewal, E. T., Kalogrides, D., & Greenberg, E. (2012). Brown fades: The end of court-ordered school desegregation and the resegregation of American public schools. *Journal of Policy Analysis and Management, 31*(4), 876–904.

Relethford, J. H. (2008). Genetic evidence and the modern human origins debate. *Heredity, 100*(6), 555–563.

Rhind, A. H. (1862). *Thebes, its tombs and their tenants*. Longman Green.

Rhineberger, G. M., Hartmann, D. J., & Van Valey, T. L. (2005). Triangulated research designs—A justification? *Journal of Applied Sociology, os-22*(1), 56–66. https://doi.org/10.1177/19367244052200106

Richmond, E. (2012, June 11). Schools are more segregated today than during the late 1960s. *The Atlantic*. https://www.theatlantic.com/national/archive/2012/06/schools-are-more-segregated-today-than-during-the-late-1960s/258348

Rickford, R. (2016). *We are an African people: Independent education, black power, and the radical imagination*. Oxford University Press.

Riegle-Crumb, C., Moore, C., & Ramos-Wada, A. (2011). Who wants to have a career in science or math? Exploring adolescents' future aspirations by gender and race/ethnicity. *Science Education, 95*(3), 458–476. https://doi.org/10.1002/sce.20431

Risse, G. B. (1986). Imhotep and medicine—A reevaluation. *Western Journal of Medicine, 144*(5), 622.

Robins, G., & Shute, C. (1987). *The Rhind Mathematical Papyrus: An ancient Egyptian text*. British Museum Publications.

Romero, A. F. (2010). At war with the state in order to save the lives of our children: The battle of ethnic studies in Arizona. *Black Scholar, 40*(4), 7–15. https://doi.org/10.1080/00064246.2010.11413528

Rupp-Eisenreich, B. (2014). Christoph Meiners' "New Science" (1747–1810). In N. Bancel, T. David, & D. Thomas (Eds.), *The invention of race: Scientific and popular representations* (pp. 68–83). Routledge.

Rury, J. L. (2012). *Education and social change: Contours in the history of American schooling*. Routledge

Rusak, S. (1996). African art: Virginia Museum of Fine Arts. *Art Education, 49*(5), 25–48. https://doi.org/10.2307/3193610

Rutgers. (n. d.). Rutgers, Africana Studies. In memoriam: Dr. Ivan van Sertima. https://africanastudies.rutgers.edu/faculty-mainmenu-134/core-faculty/90-ivan-van-sertima-in-memoriam-1935-2009

Scholtz, M. (1941). Hippocrates' aphorisms. *California and Western Medicine, 55*(6), 308.

Sedgwick, W. T., & Tyler, H. W. (1917). *A short history of science*. The MacMillan Company.

Serageldin, I. (2013). Ancient Alexandria and the dawn of medical science. *Global Cardiology Science and Practice, 2013*(4), 1–10. https://dx.doi.org/10.5339%2Fgcsp.2013.47

Shakespeare, W. (1883). *The tragedy of Othello, the Moor of Venice*. W. Swan Sonnenschein & Company.

Shakur, T., Shakur, A., & Einenkel, W. (2003). *Tupac: Resurrection, 1971–1996*. Simon & Schuster.

Shared DNA. (2005). Cambridge University Press. http://search.credoreference.com/content/entry/cuphbe/shared_dna/0

Sharp, L. A. (2016). ESEA reauthorization: An overview of the Every Student Succeeds Act. *Texas Journal of Literacy Education, 4*(1), 9–13.

Sharrock, P. D. (2013, May). The Tantric roots of the Buddhist pantheon of Jayavarman VII. In M. J. Klokke & V. Degroot (Eds.), *Materializing Southeast Asia's past: Selected papers of the 12th international conference of the European Association of Southeast Asian Archaeologists* (Vol. 2, pp. 41–55).

Shaw, I. (Ed.). (2003). *The Oxford history of ancient Egypt*. Oxford University Press.

Shelby, T. M. (1998). *The Bayon of Angkor Thom: An architectural model of Buddhist cosmology*. The University of Alabama.

Shujaa, M. J. (1994). *Too much schooling, too little education: A paradox of Black life in White societies*. Africa World Press.

Sifford, E. F. (2019). Mexican manuscripts and the first images of Africans in the Americas. *Ethnohistory, 66*(2), 223–248. https://doi.org/10.1215/00141801-7298747

Silverstein, J. (2015, June 23). Cops bought Dylann Roof Burger King after his calm arrest: Report. *New York Daily News*. https://www.nydailynews.com/news/national/dylann-roof-burger-king-cops-meal-article-1.2267615

Simon, M., & Sidner, S. (2021, January 11). Decoding the extremist symbols and groups at the Capitol Hill insurrection. CNN. https://www.cnn.com/2021/01/09/us/capitol-hill-insurrection-extremist-flags-soh/index.html

Skelton, J. (2013). *Persuasion in antiquity: A content analysis of Ptahhotep's maxims and Lao Tzu's Tao Te Ching* (Order No. 1550573). Proquest.

Sleeter, C. E., & Grant, C. A. (1987). An analysis of multicultural education in the United States. *Harvard Educational Review, 57*(4), 421–445. https://doi.org/10.17763/haer.57.4.v810xr0v3224x316

Smedley, A., & Smedley, B. (2005). Race as biology is fiction, racism as a social problem is real: Anthropological and historical perspectives on the social construction of race. *American Psychologist, 60*(1), 16. https://doi.org/10.1037/0003-066X.60.1.16

Smedley, A., & Smedley, B. (2018). *Race in North America: Origin and evolution of a worldview*. Routledge.

Smithsonian Archives. (n.d.). 150 years of Smithsonian research in Latin America. https://siarchives.si.edu/history/featured-topics/latin-american-research/matthew-williams-stirling

Smithsonian National Museum of Natural History. (n.d.). https://naturalhistory.si.edu/

Spalinger, A. (1990). The Rhind Mathematical Papyrus as a historical document. *Studien zur Altägyptischen Kultur, 17*, 295–337.

Sprunt, W. H. (1955). *Imhotep*. Mass Medical Society.

Stake, R. E. (1995). *The art of case study research*. Sage Publications.

Standerfer, L. (2006). Before NCLB: The history of ESEA. *Principal Leadership, 6*(8), 26–27.

Stanford, K. L. (2011). Keepin' it real in hip hop politics: A political perspective of Tupac Shakur. *Journal of Black Studies, 42*(1), 3–22.

Stirling, M. W. (1943). Stone monuments of southern Mexico. *Bureau of American Ethnology Bulletin, 138*, 1–84. Smithsonian Institution.

Stirling, M. W. (1955). Stone monuments of the Rio Chiquito, Veracruz, Mexico. *Bureau of American Ethnology Bulletin, 157*, 9–23. Smithsonian Institution.

Suzuki, D. T. (1960). *Manual of Zen Buddhism*. Grove Press.

Suzuki, D. T. (1991). *An introduction to Zen Buddhism*. Grove Press.

Swartz, E. E. (2013). Removing the master script: Benjamin Banneker "re-membered." *Journal of Black Studies, 44*(1), 31–49. https://doi.org/10.1177/0021934712464052

Talley-Matthews, S., & Wiggan, G. (2018). Culturally sustaining pedagogy: How teachers can teach the new majority in public schools. *Black History Bulletin, 81*(2), 24–27. https://doi.org/10.5323/blachistbull.81.2.0024

Tatum, B. D. (2007). *Can we talk about race? And other conversations in an era of school resegregation.* Beacon Press.

Teasdell, A., & Wiggan, G. (2022). Student achievement for all: Abolitionist curriculum and pedagogy to promote equity and excellence in education. In C. Lewis, S. Thomas, & S. Lee (Eds.), *Economic, political, and legal solutions to critical issues in urban education and implications for teacher preparation.* Information Age Publishing.

Thatcher, J. B. (1903). *Christopher Columbus: His life, his works, his remains: As revealed by original printed and manuscript records, together with an essay on Peter Martyr of Anghera and Bartolomé de las Casas, the first historians of America* (Vol. 2). G. P. Putnam's Sons.

Thies, C. G. (2002). A pragmatic guide to qualitative historical analysis in the study of international relations. *International Studies Perspectives, 3*(4), 351–372. https://doi.org/10.1111/1528-3577.t01-1-00099

Thompson, F. J., Wong K. K., and Rabe, B. G. (2020). *Trump, the administrative presidency, and federalism.* Brookings Institution Press.

TIMSS. (2019). International results in mathematics and science. https://timssandpirls.bc.edu/timss2019/

Tishkoff, S. A., Reed, F. A., Friedlaender, F. R., Ehret, C., Ranciaro, A., Froment, A., Hirbo, J. B., Awomoyi, A. A., Bodo, J.-M., Doumbo, O., Ibrahim, M., Juma, A. T., Kotze, M. J., Lema, G., Moore, J. H., Mortensen, H., Nyambo, T. B., Omar, S. A., Powell, K., . . . Williams, S. M. (2009). The genetic structure and history of Africans and African Americans. *Science, 324*(5930), 1035–1044. https://doi.org/10.1126/science.1172257

Truth, S. (1998). *Narrative of Sojourner Truth.* Penguin. (Original work published 1850)

Tuxteco Regional Museum. (n.d.). https://www.inah.gob.mx/museos/225-museo-tuxteco?highlight=WyJ0dXh0ZWNvIl0=

2PAC, 2PAC png. (n.d.). https://www.pngegg.com/en/png-wyxja

Ubelaker, D. H., & Angel, J. L. (1974). *Analysis of hull bay skeletons, St. Thomas.* Smithsonian Institution.

United Nations. (2022). World population to reach 8 billion on 15 November 2022. https://www.un.org/en/desa/world-population-reach-8-billion-15-november-2022

U.S. Census. (2020). Percentage distribution of race groups: 2010 and 2020. https://www.census.gov/quickfacts/fact/table/US/RHI125219#RHI125219

U.S. Census. (2021). United States Census quick facts. https://www.census.gov/quickfacts/fact/table/US/PST045221

U.S. Census Bureau. (2015). Projections of the size and composition of the U.S. population: 2014 to 2060. Population estimates and projections. https://www.census.gov/content/dam/Census/library/publications/2015/demo/p25-1143.pdf

U.S. Commission on Civil Rights. (2010). Encouraging minority students to pursue science, technology, engineering, and math careers: A briefing before the United States Commission on Civil Rights. Washington, DC.

U.S. Department of Education. (2016). *Advancing diversity and inclusion in higher education: Data highlights focusing on race and ethnicity and promising practices.* Office of Planning, Evaluation and Policy Development, Office of the Under Secretary.

U.S. Department of Education. (2021, November 26). Pending cases currently under investigation at elementary–secondary and post-secondary schools as of November 26, 2021, 7:30am. https://www2.ed.gov/about/offices/list/ocr/docs/investigations/open-investigations/tvi.html

U.S. National Library of Medicine. (2012, February 7). Hippocratic oath. https://www.nlm.nih.gov/hmd/greek/greek_oath.html

Van De Mieroop, M. (2021). *A history of ancient Egypt*. John Wiley & Sons.

Van Middendorp, J. J., Sanchez, G. M., & Burridge, A. L. (2010). The Edwin Smith Papyrus: A clinical reappraisal of the oldest known document on spinal injuries. *European Spine Journal, 19*(11), 1815–1823. https://doi.org/10.1007/s00586-010-1523-6

Van Sertima, I. (1983). *Blacks in science: Ancient and modern*. Transaction Publishers.

Van Sertima, I. (1984). *Black women in antiquity*. Transaction Publishers.

Van Sertima, I. (Ed.). (1985). *African presence in early Europe*. Transaction Publishers.

Van Sertima, I. (Ed.). (1987). *African presence in early America*. Transaction Publishers.

Van Sertima, I. (1988). *Great Black leaders: Ancient and modern*. Transaction Publishers.

Van Sertima, I., & Rashidi, R. (1985). *African presence in early Asia*. Transaction Publishers.

Van Sertima, I., & Rashidi, R. (1988). *African presence in early Asia* (rev. ed.). Transaction Publishers.

Van Sertima, I. (Ed.). (1994). *Egypt: Child of Africa*. Transaction Publishers.

Van Sertima, I. (2003). *They came before Columbus: The African presence in ancient America*. Random House Trade Paperbacks. (Original work published 1976)

Vaughan, D. B. (2021, September 10). NC Gov. Cooper vetoes anti-Critical Race Theory bill he calls conspiracy-laden politics. *Charlotte News & Observer*. https://www.newsobserver.com/news/politics-government/article253948433.html

Vaughn, L. (1998). Ancient Nubian Blacks in the Western world. *Los Angeles Sentinel, 64*(14).

Vincent, G. E. (1904). The laws of Hammurabi. *American Journal of Sociology, 9*(6), 737–754.

Wallis, C. (2020, June 12). "Why racism, not race, is a risk factor for dying of COVID-19." *Scientific American*. https://www.scientificamerican.com/article/why-racism-not-race-is-a-risk-factor-for-dying-of-covid-191/

Watkins, W. H. (2001). *The White architects of Black education: Ideology and power in America, 1865–1954*. Teachers College Press.

Watson-Vandiver, M., & Wiggan, G. (2018). The genius of Imhotep: An exploration of African-centered curricula and teaching in a high achieving U.S. urban school. *Teaching and Teacher Education, 76*(1), 151–164. https://doi.org/10.1016/j.tate.2018.09.001

Watson-Vandiver, M. J., & Wiggan, G. (2020). An environment of excellence: A case study examining a high-performing African American urban school's learning climate and approach to critical cultural care. *Journal of Education, 201*(1). https://doi.org/10.1177/0022057420904376

Watson-Vandiver, M. J., & Wiggan, G. (2021). *The healing power of education: Afrocentric pedagogy as a tool for restoration and liberation.* Teachers College Press.

Waxman, O. B. (2022, August 22). African American history finally gets its own AP class—And historians say it's more important than ever. *Time.* https://time.com/6207652/ap-african-american-history-class/

Weiant, C. (1977, May 1). Letters to the editor. *New York Times.*

Weircinski, A. (1972). Inter- and intrapopulational racial differentiation of Tlatilco Cerro de las Mesas, Teotihuacan, Monte Alban and Yucatan Maya. *Swiatowit, 32*, 175.

Wells-Barnett, I. B. (1895). *The red record: Tabulated statistics and alleged causes of lynching in the United States.* Tredition.

Wells-Barnett, I. B. (2021). *Mob rule in New Orleans: Robert Charles & his fight to death, the story of his life, burning human beings alive, & other lynching statistics-with introductory chapters by Irvine Garland Penn and T. Thomas Fortune.* Read Books. (Original work published 1900)

Wicke, C. (1965). *Olmec: An early art style of Pre-Columbia Mexico.* ProQuest Dissertations Publishing. http://search.proquest.com/docview/302128773/

Wiggan, G. (2007). Race, school achievement, and educational inequality: Toward a student-based inquiry perspective. *Review of Educational Research, 77*(3), 310–333. https://doi.org/10.3102/003465430303947

Wiggan, G. (2008). From opposition to engagement: Lessons from high achieving African American students. *The Urban Review, 40*(4), 317–349. https://doi.org/10.1007/s11256-007-0067-5

Wiggan, G. (2010). Afrocentricity and the Black intellectual tradition and education: Carter G. Woodson, W. E. B. Du Bois, and E. Franklin Frazier. *Journal of Pan African Studies, 3*(9), 128–150. https://link.gale.com/apps/doc/A306596739/LitRC?u=char69915&sid=LitRC&xid=65396105

Wiggan, G. (Ed.). (2011a). *Education for the new frontier: Race, education and triumph in Jim Crow America (1867–1945).* Nova Science Publishers.

Wiggan, G. (Ed.). (2011b). *Power, privilege, and education: Pedagogy, curriculum, and student outcomes.* Nova Science Publishers.

Wiggan, G. (2015). *In search of a canon: European history and the imperialist state.* Springer.

Wiggan, G. (2021). Black health and wellness—Race is a social construction, but racism is real. *Black History Bulletin, 84*(2), 29–34. https://doi.org/10.1353/bhb.2021.0003

Wiggan, G., Pass, M. B., & Gadd, S. R. (2020). Critical race structuralism: The role of science education in teaching social justice issues in urban education and pre-service teacher education programs. *Urban Education*. https://doi.org/10.1177/0042085920937756

Wiggan, G., Scott, L., Watson, M., & Reynolds, R. (2014). *Unshackled: Education for freedom, student achievement, and personal emancipation*. Sense Publishers.

Wiggan, G., Teasdell, A., King, L. J., Murray, A., & James-Gallaway, A. (2022). Countering miseducation: Situating K–12 social studies education within the Black intellectual tradition. *International Journal of Qualitative Studies in Education*, 1–24. https://doi.org/10.1080/09518398.2022.2025496

Wiggan, G., & Watson-Vandiver, M. (2019a). Pedagogy of empowerment: Student perspectives on critical multicultural education at a high-performing African American school. *Race, Ethnicity, and Education, 22*(6), 767–787. https://doi.org/10.1080/13613324.2017.1395328

Wiggan, G., & Watson-Vandiver, M. (2019b). Urban school success: Lessons from a high-achieving urban school, and students' reactions to Ferguson, Missouri. *Education and Urban Society, 51*(8), 1074–1105. https://doi.org/10.1177/0013124517751721

Wilder, C. S. (2013). *Ebony and ivy: Race, slavery, and the troubled history of America's universities*. Bloomsbury Publishing USA.

Wilson, J. A. (1952). A note on the Edwin Smith Surgical Papyrus. *Journal of Near Eastern Studies, 11*(1), 76–80. https://doi.org/10.1086/371061

Wilson, W. J. (2012). *The truly disadvantaged: The inner city, the underclass, and public policy*. University of Chicago Press.

Wong, K. K. (2020). Education policy Trump style: The administrative presidency and deference to states in ESSA implementation. *Publius: The Journal of Federalism, 50*(3), 423–445. https://doi.org/10.1093/publius/pjaa016

Woodson, C. G. (2006). *The miseducation of the Negro*. Book Tree. (Original work published 1933)

World Health Organization. (2020). Naming the coronavirus disease (COVID-19) and the virus that causes it. *Brazilian Journal of Implantology and Health Sciences 2*(3).

Wynn, A., Wiggan, G., Watson-Vandiver, M. J., & Teasdell, A. (2021). *Race, class, gender, and immigrant identities in education*. Springer International Publishing.

Yazan, B. (2015). Three approaches to case study methods in education: Yin, Merriam, and Stake. *The Qualitative Report, 20*(2), 134–152. https://nsuworks.nova.edu/tqr/vol20/iss2/12

Zevin, J. (2015). *Social studies for the twenty-first century: Methods and materials for teaching in middle and secondary schools* (4th ed.). Routledge.

Zinn, H., & Stefoff, R. (2009). *A young people's history of the United States* (Enhanced omnibus/paperback ed.). Seven Stories Press.

Index

Africa, xxii, xxiii, 7–9, 14, 25, 29, 66, 73, 80–81, 85–87, 91, 96, 97, 100, 105, 112–113
Ahmes I, xxiii, 33, 34, 36, 38, 40, 42–44
the Ahmes Papyrus, xxii–xxiii, 33, 34, 35, 36–38, 40–45, 48, 54, 99
the Americas, xxiv, 7, 61–75, 105
Angelou, Maya, 15
Ardi, 86
Aristotle, 17, 113
Asia, xxiv, 66, 75, 77–97

Benga, Ota, 6
Biden, President Joseph, xx, 108, 112
#BlackLivesMatter, xx
bleaching, xviii, xxii, 1, 3, 7–8, 11, 34–35, 53, 55, 57, 82, 91, 94, 109
The Book of the Coming Forth by Day, 2, 79, 105

Caucasian, 4
Clarke, John Henrik, xxiii, 7, 25, 33, 61, 65, 66, 68, 99
colossal head, 62–63, 67–68, 72–73, 75
core competencies, 23
corrected curriculum, xvi, xxiii, 16, 45, 47, 54, 56, 58, 60, 61, 74, 78, 87, 99–100
COVID-19, xv, 39, 102, 107–108, 112

critical race structuralism (CRS), xx, 20–21, 103
critical race theory (CRT), xix, xx, xxi, 13, 20–21, 101, 103, 104, 110
culturally responsive pedagogy, xvi, 15, 24, 100
culturally responsive teaching, 60, 107
curriculum reform, xiv, xxiv, 1, 15, 47, 100, 103
curriculum standards, 13, 22, 24, 70, 78, 100, 113, 114
curriculum violence, ix, xvii, xxiii, 11, 49, 59, 77, 99, 102, 111

Dancing Girl, 94–95
dehumanize, xvii, xix, xxi, 5, 6, 7, 15, 83, 104
Dinkinesh, 53, 87, 90. *See also* Lucy
Diodorus, 18–19, 77, 79–82, 84–85, 87–90, 94, 96–97
diversity, xiii, xiv–xvi, xxiii, 11, 15, 27, 37–38, 40, 56, 71, 86, 92, 100, 110
diversity, equity, and inclusion (DEI), ix, xv–xxi, xxiii, xxiv, 1, 10, 11, 14, 16, 18, 21, 22, 23, 25, 27, 29, 30, 33, 35, 36, 37, 39, 40, 45, 47–54, 56–57, 59–60, 62, 65, 69–71, 74, 75, 77, 78, 83, 100, 104, 106, 108–113, 115

DNA, xxi, 1, 9, 10, 11, 36, 42, 85–86, 105, 113
dysconscious racism, xvii, xviii, 4, 30, 106

Edelman, Marian Wright, 5, 33
"El Negro," 63
"El Rey," 62, 63, 72
Egypt, xxii, 17, 18, 29, 49, 54, 57, 77, 80, 82, 87, 88, 114
equity, xiii, xv, xvi, xviii, xx, 5, 13, 16, 20, 37, 40, 47, 57–58, 74, 97, 101–102, 104, 106, 108, 110, 115
Ethiopia, xxi, xxii, 7–9, 36, 53, 62, 63, 65, 72, 73, 79, 80, 82, 85–86, 89–91, 96, 105
Eurocentrism, xvii, xviii, xix, xxii, xxiii, xxiv, 10–11, 13, 14, 18, 21, 37, 41, 83, 104–106, 111
Europe, xix, xxii, xxiv, 9, 49, 66, 75, 77–80, 83, 85, 87–89, 91, 96–97, 99

falsification, xvii, xviii, xix, 11, 14, 48, 59, 99, 105, 111
falsify, xvii, xviii, 10, 15, 35, 38, 83, 104
Floyd, George, xix, xx, 3, 7, 112

Garvey, Marcus, xiii
Gay, Geneva, xvi, 16, 25, 41, 56, 59, 60, 70, 74, 75, 78, 100, 103, 109
Gudea, 92–94

Harris, Vice President Kamala D., xx, 108, 112
healing, xiii, xiv, xx, 4–5, 9, 13, 53, 57, 59–60, 82
hegemony, xvi, xxii, 7, 15, 21, 23, 37, 40, 51, 86, 111
Herodotus, 9, 16–18, 77, 79, 80, 84, 85, 88–89, 91, 94, 96, 97, 113
Hertslet, Edward, 7
Hilliard, Asa G., III, xi, xiii, xvi, xxiii, 4, 13, 16, 19, 25, 27, 28, 33, 47, 48
Hippocrates, 48, 49, 56, 57, 113

Homer, 18, 19, 82
hooks, bell, xiv, 100, 109, 111
Human Family Tree, xvii, xxi, 1, 5, 41, 53, 100, 101

Imhotep, xxii–xxiv, 16, 38, 40, 45, 47–60, 61, 91, 99, 105, 112, 113
inclusion, ix, xii, xv–xvii, xxiii, 11, 13, 15–16, 22, 25, 33, 35, 37, 47, 54, 59, 62–65, 71, 74–75, 97, 100, 109, 111–113, 115
Indigenous, 7–8, 34, 54, 63–64, 68
instruction, xv, xvi, xviii, xxi, 14, 20, 24, 30, 47, 72, 99, 102, 107–109
internalized domination, xvii, 1, 12, 13

Kemet, xxii, 16–18, 63
King, Joyce E., xviii, 12, 37, 59

The Law of Hammurabi, 79
Lucy, 53, 85, 86, 90. *See also* Dinkinesh

Mandela, Nelson, 1
Map of Africa by Treaty, 7
marginalize, xvii, 10, 15, 83, 84, 104, 113
MDW-NTR, 19, 26–28, 55, 105
miseducation, ix, xviii, xxiii, 8, 11, 12, 15, 29, 44, 49, 59, 69, 70, 71, 75, 78, 99, 111
The Miseducation of the Negro, 29
multicultural, ix, xix, 10, 14, 18, 23, 30, 33, 36, 40, 41, 44, 45, 48, 58–60, 61, 66, 71, 77, 78, 83, 84, 104, 110, 112–113
multiculturalism, xiv, xviii, 11, 12, 18, 22, 78, 104, 111
multicultural strategies, ix, xiv

National Assessment of Educational Progress (NAEP), xiv, 106, 107
National Center for Education Statistics (NCES), xiv, xv, xvi, 39
National Council for the Social Studies, 16, 65, 78

National Curriculum Standards for Social Studies, 16, 20, 44, 65, 70
The Nation's Report Card, xv, 106

Obama, President Barack, xx, 107, 108
Olmec, xxiv, 61–75, 84, 99, 105, 112–113
omissions, ix, xiv, xvi, xxiv, 12, 14, 22, 29, 37, 48, 49, 61, 70, 77, 78, 87, 97, 99, 100, 112
oppression, xiv, xvii, xx, xxi, 8, 9, 10, 11, 13, 15, 20, 21, 29, 48, 53, 83, 97, 104, 105

Plato, 17, 18, 19, 114
power, ix, xiii, xiv, xvii–xx, 2, 3, 5, 7, 10, 11, 13, 15, 23, 29, 48, 54, 56, 59, 83, 87, 94, 100, 102, 103–106, 108
privilege, ix, xvii, xix, xx, 1–3, 8, 10, 11, 15, 23, 29, 48, 54, 83, 100, 102–104, 106, 112
PtahHotep, xxii, xxiii, 14, 15–31, 33, 36, 42, 48, 49, 79, 99, 105, 112, 113

racism as a mental health disorder, 5
Rhind, xxiii, 34–35, 37, 42–44, 47, 54, 99, 105
right knowledge, xxiii, 48, 59, 60
Rogers, Joel Augustus, 37

#SayHerName Movement, xx
school reform, xiii, xv, 103, 106–108
Senusret, 80
Senwosret, 80
Sesostris, 79–81, 87–89
1619 Project, 101, 104
skin bleaching, 1, 3, 8, 11
Smith, Edwin, xxiii, 54–57, 91, 105

social studies, 13, 16, 17, 19, 20, 22–25, 29–31, 35, 36, 40, 44, 61, 65, 69–71, 74, 75, 77, 78, 79, 83, 90, 92, 94, 97, 105, 106, 114
STEM, 33, 38, 39, 45, 47–49, 56–59, 108
STEM/STEAM, 35, 36, 38, 40, 47–51, 54, 57, 58
Stirling, Matthew, 62–65, 68, 69, 71, 72, 74
suppressions, xvii, 61

The Teachings of PtahHotep, xxiii, 14, 15–16, 18–20, 22, 23, 25–31, 48, 79, 105
Truth, Sojourner, 7
Tupac, xxiii, 47, 50–54, 56–57, 59–60

unbleaching, ix, xiv, xvi–xxiv, 1, 4, 7, 9–23, 25, 27, 29–31, 33, 35–38, 40–45, 48, 49, 51, 54, 59–62, 65–66, 68–69, 71–72, 74–75, 78, 79, 82–83, 85, 91, 92, 96–97, 99–106, 108–115
undermine, xvii, 10, 15, 64, 78, 83, 102, 104
unlearn, 2
unlearning, 2

Wells Barnett, Ida B., xi
whiten up, xxiii, 54
whitening up, xvii, xxii, 65, 99
whitewashed, ix, 7, 8, 15, 19, 42, 48, 77, 96, 97, 103, 112, 114
whitewashing, xvii, xviii, xxii, 8, 9, 14, 34, 49, 51, 55, 57, 58, 62, 64–66, 74, 78, 91, 94, 99, 105, 109, 111, 113
Woodson, Carter G., xi, xviii, 29, 37, 69

About the Authors

Greg Wiggan is professor of urban education, adjunct professor of sociology, and affiliate faculty of Africana studies at the University of North Carolina at Charlotte. His research addresses school processes that promote high achievement among urban and minority students. He was the recipient of the 2015 Cato College of Education Award for Excellence in Teaching and the College's Diversity Award. He is a nationally award-nominated author and has published over 100 publications, inclusive of 30 education books, with notable titles such as *Global Issues in Education*; *Power, Privilege and Education*; *Teacher Education to Enhance Diversity in STEM*; *Sister Outsider in the Academy*; and *The Healing Power of Education*. His work appears in more than 70 countries and over 6,000 college and university libraries (WorldCat, 2022), including prestigious outlets listed in *U.S. News and World Report*.

Annette Teasdell is assistant professor of curriculum and instruction at Clark Atlanta University and the coordinator of the Master of Arts in Special Education Program. She holds a doctorate in curriculum and instruction with an emphasis in urban education from UNC Charlotte. Her research agenda is driven by her commitment to improving academic outcomes for students in urban schools and communities through curriculum development. Additionally, her research is centered on the fundamental belief that culturally responsive pedagogy combined with a curriculum that is accurate, relevant, and appropriate, and whose educational processes are humane, can yield improved student outcomes. She is the co-author of *Race, Class, Gender, and Immigrant Identities in Education: Perspectives from First and Second Generation Ethiopian Students*.

Marcia J. Watson-Vandiver is associate professor of elementary education at Towson University. She attended Mercer University in Macon, Georgia, where she received her BS in middle grades education with specializations in language arts and social studies methods. She received her MEd in educational policy and leadership from Georgia State University. She later received her PhD in curriculum and instruction–urban education and a graduate certificate in Africana studies from the University of North Carolina at Charlotte. Marcia is the co-author of *Unshackled: Education for Freedom, Student Achievement, and Personal Emancipation* and the co-editor of *Contemporary African American Families: Achievements, Challenges, and Empowerment Strategies in the 21st Century*. Her research interests explore various intersections of Black education, including resistance pedagogy, historical and contemporary issues in urban education, critical multiculturalism, and transformative/emancipatory learning.

Sheikia Talley-Matthews is an educational researcher who holds a doctorate in curriculum and instruction from the University of North Carolina at Charlotte. She is the author of *Sister Outsider in the Academy: Untold Stories of Afro-Caribbean Women in United States Colleges and Universities*. She is also a former high school history teacher who holds a master's in secondary social studies education and a bachelor's in history.

Ingram Content Group UK Ltd.
Milton Keynes UK
UKHW011551160523
421837UK00003B/19